GALATIANS: Treasure Hunt for Freedom

David W. Welday III, *publisher*
Jim Kochenburger, *managing editor*
Paul Allen, *editor*
Rebecca Ussery, Laurie Dickerson, Patsy Cockrum, Nancy Price, Donna Winsor, *writers*

Kathleen Stemley, *cover design*

ACTIVITY ZONE

Greg Cross, Kathleen Stemley, *Activity Zone artists*

Scriptures quoted from the *International Children's Bible, New Century Version,* copyright ©1986, 1988 by Word Publishing, Dallas, Texas 75039. Used by permission.

©1998 CharismaLife Publishers
600 Rinehart Road · Lake Mary, FL 32746
Editorial Offices: (407) 333-7303
Toll-Free Order Line: (800) 451-4598
www.CharismaLife.com
ISBN 1-57405-398-1

All rights reserved. No part of this book may be reproduced in any manner whatsoever without written permission from the publisher, except where noted. For information, write to the Copyrights/Permissions Assistant.

We want to hear from you. If you have any comments, questions or suggestions, please write to the CharismaLife Editorial Department. We reserve the right to publish letters addressed to CharismaLife Publishers.

If you wish to submit new product ideas, articles or manuscripts, please write to the CharismaLife Editorial Department.

Mission Statement

Equip the body of Christ to bring children and youth into the kingdom and train them to walk and minister in the power of the Holy Spirit.

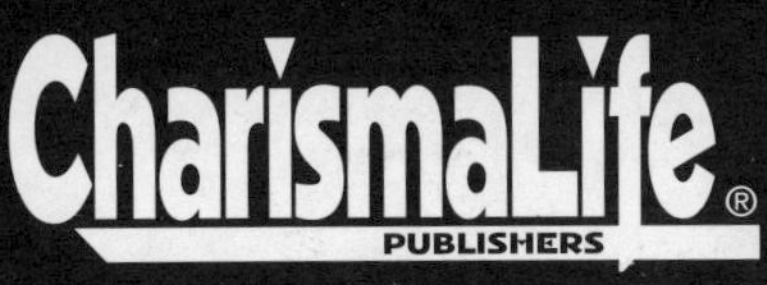

TABLE OF CONTENTS

TEACHER HELP PAGES

A Letter From the Editor...

Dear Club 56 Leaders,

We all enjoy a treasure hunt, especially when we know the treasure is for something we will benefit from once we find it. This quarter we are going to be studying the book of Galatians. In it we will discover that Paul is explaining to the Galatians that salvation is a free gift from God, not something that can be purchased.

It will be important for us to help our students understand the terms of grace and how they apply to our lives. Likewise, we can show them how God provided for us the fruit of the Spirit and the gifts of the Spirit that enable us to serve Him faithfully.

Donald G. Barnhouse, a former pastor of 10th Street Presbyterian Church in Philadelphia, once explained the fruit of the Spirit in an interesting manner. He explained how each fruit mentioned was a characteristic of the first word, love.

JOY is love singing in our lives.
PEACE is the ability for love to have rest.
LONG SUFFERING is love enduring in every situation.
GENTLENESS is love's true touch towards others.
GOODNESS is love's character in our actions.
FAITH is love's habit established in our everyday lives.
MEEKNESS is love's self-forgetfulness in thinking of others.
SELF CONTROL is love holding the reigns so that Christ would have control.

As we walk together through this study, let's pray together for God's Spirit to touch our students afresh with His love and power. We can help them find that freedom they need to allow the Holy Spirit to begin a new work in their lives and touch our nation through their faithfulness to Him.

Discovering His Freedom,

Paul Allen
Club 56 Editor

COMPONENTS OF CLUB 56

Title Page

Power Point — This is the main point you will emphasize throughout the Bible Lesson, activities and Challenge.

Memory Verse — You and your students will learn this verse through a fun activity.

Lesson Scripture — Read this section of Scripture to see what will be covered in the Bible Lesson.

Bible Lesson Outline — This three- or four-point brief overview of the Bible Lesson helps you remember the points to go over as you teach.

Teacher Devotion — This section shows how the Power Point can impact **your** life. Written from experiences in the writers' lives, these devotions will help you see clearly that this lesson is not only for 5th and 6th graders, but also for you.

Extra Helps

Pastoring Tip — Each lesson has pastoring tips to help you identify ways to minister to, care for and direct the 5th and 6th graders in their relationships with the Lord.

Teacher Help — Short notes to give you further direction in activities for either large or small classes, to instruct you in practical wisdom about 5th and 6th graders or to point out safety considerations during an activity.

Power Point — The Power Point is repeated throughout each lesson to help you remember the focus.

Memory Verse — The Memory Verse appears in the column next to the Memory Verse Activity.

The Lesson

Challenge Review — This section (in Lessons 2-13) will help reinforce the Power Point or Memory Verse from the week before, using the Challenge your students were given.

Opening Activity — A fun, hands-on activity that will get the kids immediately involved in the focus of the Bible Lesson.

Bible Lesson — The interactive Bible Lesson will cover three or four main points from the Lesson Scripture that will help your students understand how the Scripture applies to their lives.

Memory Verse Activity — Fun activities for 5th and 6th graders that help your students memorize the Scripture and learn what it means for them.

More Activities — Four additional fun activities that go along with the Power Point and Bible Lesson. There are a variety of activities so that every kind of learner can enjoy the activity time.

Living It Out — A current-day, open-ended situation that your class will resolve together.

Challenge for the Week — The Challenge helps bridge a student's home with your Sunday School class. Students work on the Challenge over the week and bring it back to discuss the following week.

Club 56 Activity Zone — A full-color book that has two of the activities for each lesson. Order one for each student by calling CharismaLife Publishers, 1-800-451-4598.

ITEMS NEEDED FOR LESSON

❑ Newspapers (one for every two students)

❑ Bibles
❑ Copies of *Club 56 Leader's Manual* page 14 (or map of Paul's missionary journeys)
❑ Life Savers (three variety rolls)
❑ Blindfolds (two)
❑ Paper
❑ Pencils
❑ Chalkboard
❑ Chalk

❑ Balloons (16)
❑ Strips of paper (16, small)
❑ Posterboard
❑ Pens
❑ Candy (assorted, one bag)

❑ None

1—Creative Writing

❑ *Club 56 Activity Zone* page 1
❑ Pencils

2—Individual Art

❑ *Club 56 Activity Zone* page 2
❑ Colored pencils

3—Problem Solving

❑ None

4—Object Lesson

❑ World map (large)
❑ Pins (straight)
❑ Bulletin board
❑ String

❑ Copies of Lesson 1 Secret Orders

SPECIAL NOTE

As you begin this quarter, ask the Holy Spirit to direct your teaching toward the needs of your students. Kids today need a better grasp on God's grace and what it means in their lives.

Regarding the challenge for this study, take time to discuss the activities and provide a 3-prong folder for each child. It will be something for them to keep and look at down the road on their spiritual journey.

Discover God by knowing Jesus.

I said this before. Now I say it again: You have already accepted the Good News. If anyone tells you another way to be saved, he should be condemned!

Galatians 1:9

John 3:16; Acts 16:30-31; 1 Corinthians 15:1-4; Galatians 1:1-9; 2:16-21;

A. A Prolific Writer
B. A Serious Problem
C. Anyone For a Life Saver?
D. By the Book
E. In the Good Ol' 20th Century

HUNTING FOR TRUE SALVATION

Some People Get It, Some People Don't

Several years ago as I was praying, the Lord impressed these words on me: "You are afraid of grace." I was astounded. I had walked with Him for a number of years, been a children's pastor for ten years and thought I was following God in every way I could. How could I be afraid of grace?

Over the ensuing weeks and months, the Lord began to show me what He meant. My thinking about quiet times came under His scrutiny. Although I enjoyed spending time with Him, my thinking had become that of having a quiet time in order to have my day go well. It was a subtle but profound error in thinking—if I did something correctly, God would be with me.

A friend was sharing his struggle with this same thing a couple of weeks ago. He was driving on the freeway one day, felt an urgency to pray and found himself slowing down to the speed limit so that God would listen. His thinking was that if he wanted something from God, he must follow the letter of the law.

I think most of us are afraid of grace at different points in our lives. We're afraid that God doesn't really mean it when He says there is absolutely no way we can please Him through our own efforts. As a matter of fact, God knows there is nothing good in us. With our best intentions in place, we still will fail.

As you prepare to teach this lesson on salvation and grace, be available to the Holy Spirit to recognize times when you slip into keeping the law in order to be right with God. Release those things and move back into grace. Your kids need to see and sense your lifestyle of grace.

Materials: Newspapers (one for every two students).

Today we begin an adventure in the book of Galatians. The subtitle for our 13 lessons is "Treasure Hunt for Freedom." We're going to begin our lesson today with a treasure hunt in the newspaper. With a partner, you need to find three examples of people doing a really good or a really bad activity. You need to include at least one example of each. Answer this question about each of the people whose examples you chose: Is that person a Christian? How do you know?

Give the students five minutes to look through the paper to choose examples. Gather the class and have each pair share their three examples and their answers to the questions posed. Accept all answers.

You found some great examples. At the end of our lesson, I'm going to ask you the same questions about these people. Let's see if your answers change or remain the same.

Get involved

Materials: Copies of *Club 56 Leader's Manual* page 14 (or map of Paul's missionary journeys), Bibles, Life Savers candy (three variety rolls), blindfolds (two), paper, pencils, chalkboard and chalk.

Before class: Unwrap two rolls and sort candy by flavors. Save one roll to give as a prize. Write down the flavors in the order you will give them out. See the game instructions under "Anyone for a Life Saver?" Make enough copies of the map for each student to have one.

A Prolific Writer

Today we begin a study in the book of Galatians. Galatians was written by Paul.

♦ **What other books in the New Testament were written by him?** *(Have students look in their Bibles at the first verse of each book. Paul's name is in the books he wrote.)* Romans, 1 and 2 Corinthians, Ephesians, Philippians, Colossians, 1 and 2 Thessalonians, 1 and 2 Timothy, Titus and Philemon.

Paul wrote many letters to churches and people, which have become a part of our Bible.

Discover God by knowing Jesus.

Galatians is a book that will probably challenge your thinking about grace. Read through it several times in the coming weeks, allowing the Holy Spirit to minister to you personally about His grace.

(Hand out the maps.) Galatians was written to Christians in Galatia. Find Galatia on your maps.

♦ Is Galatia a country or a city? *Country.*

♦ Can anyone name the country today which would have Galatia in it? *Turkey.*

Paul had visited parts of Galatia and told the people about Jesus Christ. Many people were saved and began following the Lord. After Paul left, however, people who had visited Galatia informed him that the Christians there believed things other than what they had been taught about Jesus Christ. Let's dive right into the book and find out what was happening.

A Serious Problem

(Have one or two students read aloud Gal. 1:1-9.) Paul sounded concerned about the Galatians in verses 6-9.

♦ **What was he concerned about?** *That the people stopped believing the Good News. They were adding to it rather than just believing in Jesus Christ.*

The entire book of Galatians is one in which Paul deals with this one theme—that there is nothing else to add to true salvation, believing in and receiving Christ. The Galatians were being taught there was another part of salvation required that they hadn't done yet. They thought there was something they needed to do in addition to receiving Christ as their Savior! This matter was important enough for Paul to send an entire letter to these churches, and also important enough for us that the letter is included in our Bibles. The Holy Spirit must want us to remember what salvation is and is not. Let's discover together what that is.

Anyone for a Life Saver?

We're going to have a test, but not like at school. I think you'll like this test. *(Divide the students into two teams. Give one blindfold to each team. The teams should stand in lines. The first person on each team should be blindfolded.)* Your job is to taste the Life Saver I put in your mouth and tell what flavor it is. The recorder on your team will write your guess of the flavor. When you are done, you must blindfold the second person, at which time I will give him a Life Saver. He will guess the flavor and then blindfold the next person. We will continue until everyone on both teams has tasted and guessed the flavor of a Life Saver. The fastest and most accurate team will win a roll of Life Savers to share.

(Play the game, awarding five points for the first team done and one point for each correct flavor guess. Give the winning team the extra roll of Life Savers.) You all did really well at the test.

In Galatia, the test was whether the people would believe anyone who told them what they needed to do to be saved.

♦ **After reading those first few verses of Galatians, how do you think they scored on their test?** *Not very well. They believed things that weren't true about the Good News.*

The only lifesaver we need is Jesus Christ. We don't have to perform in a particular way. Believing in and receiving Jesus Christ as our personal Savior is all that's required. So, here's your test:

♦ **What do you need to do to be saved?** *Believe in and receive Jesus Christ as my personal Savior.*

By the Book

Paul said that being a Christian is believing the Good News. Let's find out what that means. I'm going to assign you a section of Scripture. *(Divide the students into four groups. Assign each group one of the following Scripture verses.)*

◊ Galatians 2:16-21

◊ 1 Corinthians 15:1-4

◊ John 3:16

◊ Acts 16:30-31

With your group, read the verses and answer these two questions:

♦ **According to these Scripture verses, who is a Christian?**

♦ **According to these Scripture verses, who is not a Christian?**

(Give them three minutes to complete the assignment. Gather the students back together and have them share their answers. Write the highlights on the chalkboard.)

Christians are people who believe that Jesus Christ is the only Son of God and that He died on the cross to forgive their sins. They are people who have received Him as their own personal Savior.

In the Good Ol' 20th Century

(Ask the students the following questions, allowing them to answer. Don't give any feedback to their answers until all the questions have been asked and answered.)

♦ **What does a Christian look like?**

♦ **What does a Christian act like?**

♦ **What kinds of words does a Christian use?**

♦ **What kinds of words should a Christian never use?**

Those questions were kind of trick questions. A Christian is a person who has received Christ, not a person who acts, talks or lives a certain way. Paul's message for the Galatians is for Club 56 members, too! We can't add to what Scripture says about salvation.

The word *Christian* is a noun. It is something you are, not something you do. It's not an adjective. It doesn't describe your behavior, clothing, personality or anything else. It simply says that you belong to God through Jesus Christ.

It's important for us to understand what Paul was saying: the one thing that makes a person a Christian is that he believes Jesus Christ is the only Son of God and receives Jesus' sacrifice for his sin. There are no other conditions—you don't have to act a certain way, use holy words or look saintly.

Let's think back to the treasure hunt in the newspapers and see if we've changed perspectives at all.

When asking questions, listen to the students' answers. Allow them to freely express different viewpoints, then lead them to see the truth from Scripture.

Discover God by knowing Jesus.

(Have each student answer the following questions about their earlier assessments of people in the newspaper.)

♦ How did you make your decisions about who was a Christian?

♦ Can a person who does something wrong be a Christian?

♦ Is every person who does something heroic or helpful a Christian?

Conclusion

In Galatians, Paul was helping the people see that the only test for who was saved was whether or not they had received Jesus Christ as their Savior—whether they believed the Good News of Christ. When other people came to tell the Galatians other things they needed to do to get salvation, the Galatians forgot they had already done everything when they received Christ. That same Good News is ours today. All we need is Jesus Christ.

♦ **How many of you have received Jesus Christ as your personal Savior?**
(Have any students who are willing to share tell when and where that happened for them. Share your own personal experience as well.)

Let's pray right now. If you have never received Jesus as your Savior, this would be a great day to do it. All you have to do is tell Him you believe in Him and want to receive His sacrifice for your sin. You can repeat this prayer after me. *(Pause where indicated to give students time to repeat what you have said.)* Dear God,/Thank You for sending Jesus/to forgive my sins. /I believe He is Your Son. /I believe He died for me. /I receive Jesus Christ into my life. /Please come and live with me by Your Holy Spirit. /In Jesus' name, amen.

If this is the first time you have asked Jesus to be your Savior, please come and tell me after our class is over. I'd like to help you begin your new life with Him.

Galatians 1:9

I said this before. Now I say it again: You have already accepted the Good News. If anyone tells you another way to be saved, he should be condemned!

Materials: Balloons (16), strips of paper (16, small), posterboard (two), pens and candy (assorted, one bag).

Before class: On the strips of paper, make two sets of the following clues:

◊ I am a sinner.

◊ I cannot earn my salvation.

◊ Jesus paid for my sins on the cross.

◊ Through my faith in Jesus Christ I will have eternal life.

◊ If I do what is right, I might be good enough to go to heaven.

◊ I'm not sure if I will go to heaven, but I hope I will.

◊ If I have enough self-discipline to stop sinning, I can go to heaven.

◊ I will be reincarnated until I reach a state of worthiness.

Place each strip in a balloon. Blow up and tie all the balloons. Make two groups of balloons. Each group should contain all eight clues.

Sometimes a story gets passed around from person to person so many times that it becomes exaggerated or even changed altogether. Most of us have had the experience of playing the telephone game. As the message is whispered from person to person, the story changes a little bit. By the time the message reaches the end of the line, it is very different from the message that was delivered in the beginning.

Paul warned the Galatians about believing a message that was different from the Good News they had first believed.

♦ **What is the Good News?** *I am a sinner. I cannot earn salvation. God sent His Son, Jesus, to die for our sins. Jesus rose from the dead on the third day.*

♦ **How do you think the message of salvation might have changed?**

Paul's warning is also for us to remember. **Let's take a minute to memorize our Memory Verse.** Allow the students to work with a partner to memorize the verse. Then call on pairs to stand up and recite the Memory Verse.

Now we are going to play a game about the Good News. You will be divided into two teams. Each team will be given a bunch of balloons and a posterboard. Each team will try to pop the balloons by stepping on them. When a balloon is popped, the team will read the clue together. If it says something that is part of the Good News, a team member will run to his team's poster and copy the sentence from the paper. If the clue is a message that is different from the Good News, the clue should be discarded. The first team to find the four parts of the Good News and write them on their posterboard wins.

Divide the class into two teams. After they have completed the game, review the basic message of the Good News. Give the winning team their choice of candy.

1—Creative Writing

Materials: *Club 56 Activity Zone* page 1 and pencils.

Today we've talked about what being a Christian means. Now I want you to write a note to three different people, telling them what your salvation means.

Find times when everyone is working on activities individually to pray quietly for each student. Ask the Holy Spirit to give you wisdom when talking with each one.

Activity Zone page 1

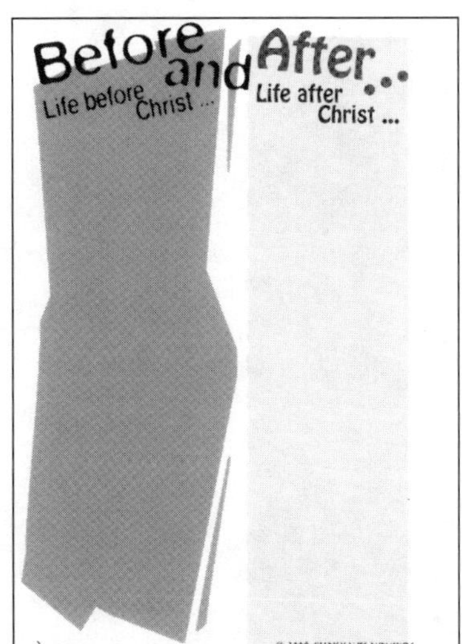

Activity Zone page 2

When explaining activities, make sure everyone understands the directions. Have someone repeat them for the class.

Discover God by knowing Jesus.

Tell them what difference Jesus has made in your life. How has His saving you been a good thing? Read the activity page and follow the instructions.

After the students have completed their pages, have them share one of their letters with the whole class.

2—Individual Art

Materials: *Club 56 Activity Zone* page 2 and colored pencils.

In our lesson today, we discovered that there is a great difference between being and not being a Christian.

♦ **What are some ways this difference could be illustrated?** *Dark and light, alive and dead, big and little, etc.*

On your activity page, there are two columns. Using your colored pencils, show the difference in one's life before and after salvation by drawing ways to represent life before Christ in one column and life after Christ in the other column.

3—Problem Solving

♦ **What is our Power Point today?** *Discover God by knowing Jesus.*

♦ **Do you know any people who have not yet discovered God by knowing Jesus?** Allow students to name some of those people.

In this activity, you will talk with one other person in class about how the Power Point could have worked in one of those people's lives. Pick someone you have played with, listened to or talked to this week and tell how, in your home or at school, that person could discover God by knowing Jesus.

4—Object Lesson

Materials: World map (large), pins (straight), bulletin board and string.

Before class: Pin the world map to the bulletin board.

I want to draw your attention to this world map. In the past, people have accomplished the feats of sailing and flying around the world. Recently people have been trying to accomplish a feat that has never been done before. They are trying to circle the globe in a hot air balloon.

♦ **What paths have they tried to take around the world?** As students provide information, place straight pins on the map at the points they discuss and then tie the string to the pins to show the courses that were taken.

♦ **The balloonists have faced many different obstacles. What are some problems they face?** *Weather, mountain ranges, balloon malfunctions, countries denying flight over their territory.*

♦ **If you were going to fly around the world, what course would you take?**

Although the balloonists knew the journey would be tough, they attempted to find ways to struggle through and earn success. In the world, many people feel the same way about knowing God and getting into heaven. They think they have to earn God's acceptance by being really good or by obeying all the laws and rules. They make salvation difficult.

Instead, we heard today that salvation is easy. It can't be earned. Jesus already paid the price. We just have to receive Christ into our lives and have a personal relationship with Him! Whew! Isn't it a relief to know we don't have to be perfect? We just have to believe in the One who is!

"Brad!" shouted Ray from across the cafeteria. Grabbing a carton of milk, Ray tossed it in the air as he made his way to where Brad was sitting. "Hey man, are you busy next Sunday?"

Brad looked at Ray and answered cautiously, "Well, I'm going to church now on Sunday, so I don't think I can do anything until afterwards. What do you want to do?"

Ray was surprised, "Why didn't you tell me about this? Where are you going to church?" Brad told him and was surprised at Ray's instant negative reaction. "Why would you go to church there? They don't have any standards at that church. They go to movies, listen to secular music and drink sodas. The girls wear jewelry and even cut their hair like boys! You know what bothers me most about them?"

Before Brad could answer, Ray continued angrily, "They just figure they can say, 'Hey, God, sorry!' and He'll say, 'No big deal.' But that isn't true. You gotta' earn your right to be a Christian. You need to show God that you deserve to go to heaven; it's no free gift!"

Ray paused for a minute and then looked embarrassed. "Well, I didn't mean to preach a sermon, Brad. I just don't want you to make a mistake."

Brad was uncomfortable because he didn't really know the Bible well enough to explain what he believed. Finally he spoke. "Well, I thought the Bible says that salvation is a free gift if you believe in Jesus."

"Yep," answered Ray, "that's just what they want you to believe. But believe me, getting saved is just the beginning of a lot of hard work to earn your right to be a Christian. You really need to talk to my pastor. He can help you understand the rules. Why don't you come to church with me Sunday?

Brad wasn't sure what to do. He wished he had someone to talk to who could tell him what he should believe.

How would you help Brad?

Divide the class into small discussion groups. Read the Memory Verse, Galatians 1:9, to the group. Ask each group to discuss the questions below. After the discussion have each group share their answers with the class.

Challenge your students' common religious phrases with, "What does that mean in your real life, Candy?"

Discover God by knowing Jesus.

♦ Why did Ray react so strongly to Brad's choice of a church?

♦ What are some of the things that bother Ray about the kids at Brad's new church?

♦ Ray said that people must earn the right to be Christians. How does that line up with the Memory Verse for today?

♦ What is the difference between making good choices as a Christian versus living by rules in order to be saved?

Materials: Copies of Lesson 1 Secret Orders.

Pssst. You. Yeah, you. Come over here. I want to talk to you. I've been watching you for awhile and you look like just the kind of "Joe" I need. I work in covert operations. You know, undercover work. Right now I'm looking for someone who could help me gather some important information. Are you game? There could be a big payoff in the end if you do your job right.

OK, here is your first assignment. Some people just don't get it. They think that being a Christian involves a lot of do's and don'ts. You are to look into some of the claims that Jesus made. Find three things He said about how to be saved. You will find that Jesus did most of His talking in the first four books of the New Testament. Those books are Matthew, Mark, Luke and John.

Remember to bring your completed Secret Orders to class next week. Happy hunting and remember...shhhh!

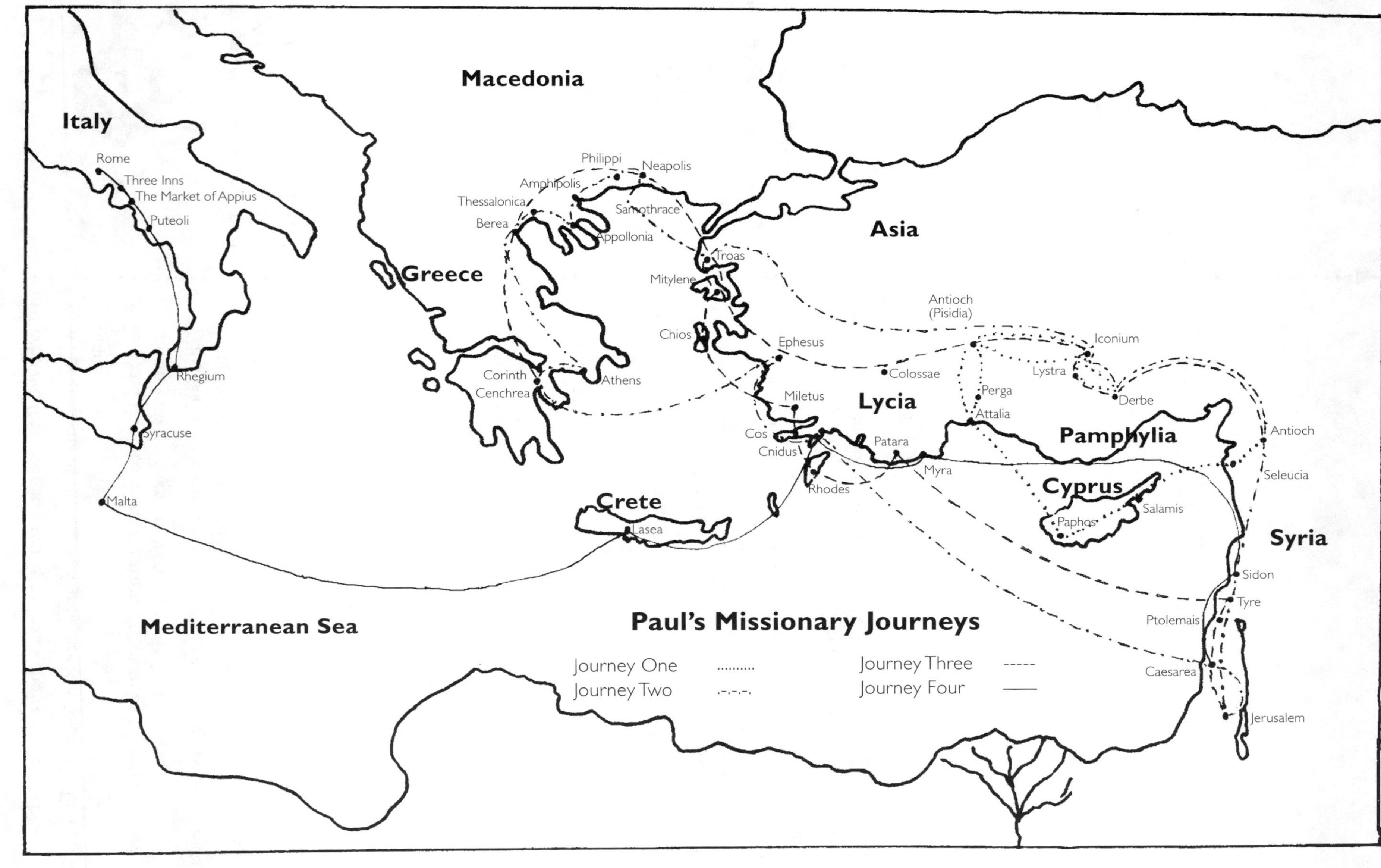

Paul's Missionary Journeys
Italy
Macedonia
Greece
Asia
Lycia
Pamphylia
Cyprus
Syria
Crete
Mediterranean Sea
Rome
Three Inns
The Market of Appius
Puteoli
Rhegium
Syracuse
Malta
Amphipolis
Philippi
Neapolis
Thessalonica
Berea
Appollonia
Samothrace
Mitylene
Troas
Chios
Corinth
Cenchrea
Athens
Ephesus
Miletus
Cos
Cnidus
Rhodes
Patara
Myra
Colossae
Antioch (Pisidia)
Perga
Attalia
Lystra
Iconium
Derbe
Antioch
Seleucia
Paphos
Salamis
Sidon
Tyre
Ptolemais
Caesarea
Jerusalem
Lasea
Journey One ....
Journey Two -..-..-
Journey Three -----
Journey Four ———

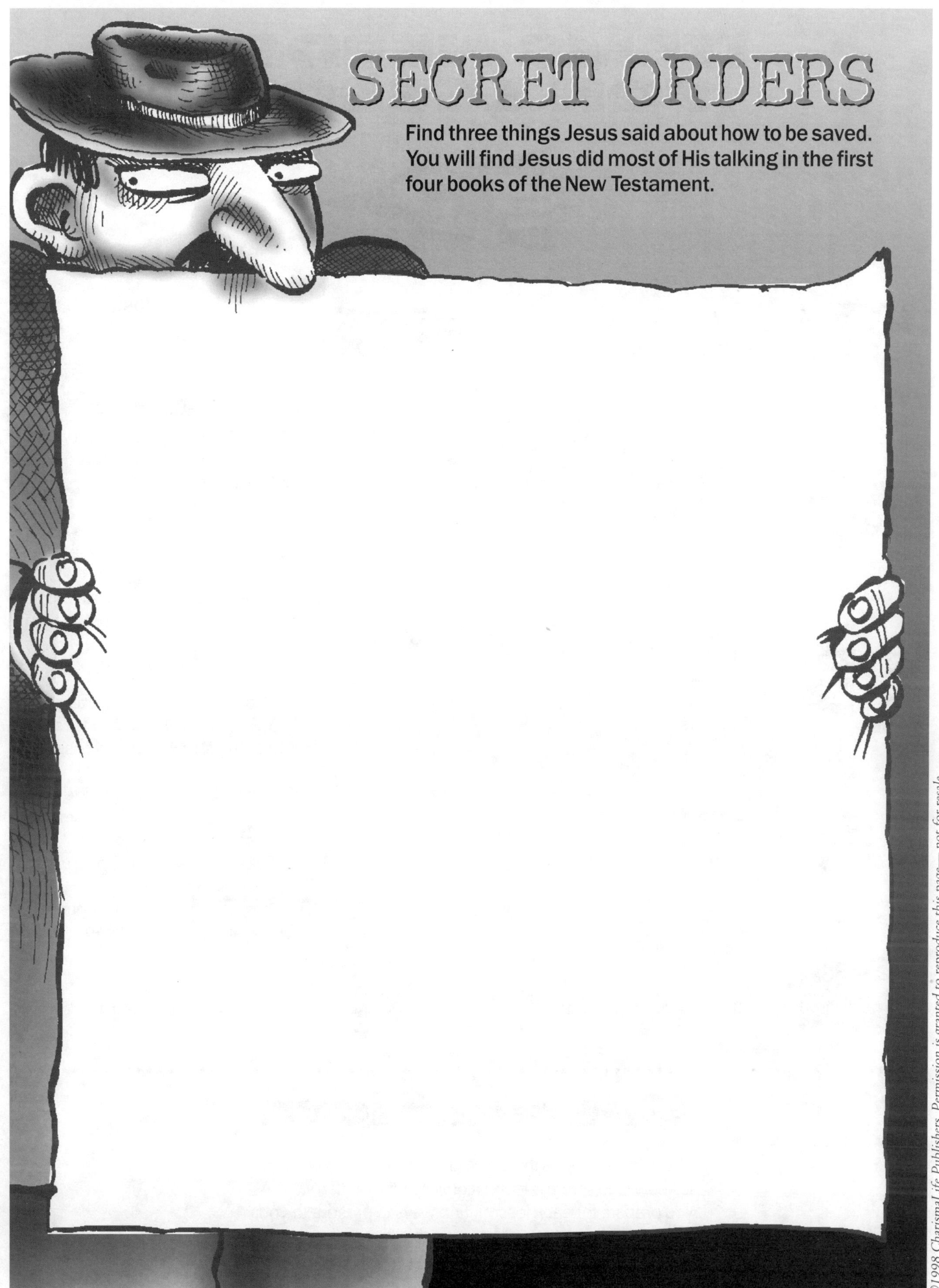

SECRET ORDERS

Find three things Jesus said about how to be saved.
You will find Jesus did most of His talking in the first
four books of the New Testament.

ITEMS NEEDED FOR LESSON

❑ Challenge notebooks
❑ Lesson 1 Secret Orders

1—Music

❑ *Club 56 Activity Zone* page 3
❑ Pencils

2—Bible Study

❑ *Club 56 Activity Zone* page 4
❑ Bibles
❑ Concordances
❑ Pencils

❑ Paper
❑ Pencils
❑ Chalkboard
❑ Chalk

3—Group Art

❑ Chalkboard
❑ Chalk
❑ Posterboard
❑ Markers
❑ Scissors
❑ Glue
❑ Construction paper

❑ Bibles
❑ Chalkboard
❑ Chalk
❑ Paper
❑ Pencils

4—Cooking

❑ Popcorn (one gallon, popped)
❑ Brown sugar (2 cups)
❑ Margarine (1 cup)
❑ Corn syrup (1/2 cup)
❑ Salt (1 teaspoon)
❑ Peanuts (small can)
❑ Pot (large)
❑ Hot plate
❑ Wooden spoon
❑ Paper bag (large)
❑ Cookie sheet
❑ Bags (small, plastic)
❑ Slips of paper
❑ Pens
❑ Aluminum foil
❑ Bibles

❑ Slips of paper
❑ Pencils
❑ Bibles

❑ Copies of Living It Out story

❑ Copies of Lesson 2 Secret Orders

SPECIAL NOTE

The world is telling us there is no absolute truth. Our kids need to know God's truth is foundational to our Christian walk. As you prepare for each lesson, find ways to present to your students the truth that will be applicable to their lives.

God's truth is nothing but the truth.

Brothers, I want you to know that the Good News I preached to you was not made by men. I did not get it from men, nor did any man teach it to me. Jesus Christ showed it to me.
Galatians 1:11-12

Isaiah 40:31; Matthew 6:31-33; John 1:32-33; 14:16-17,26; Acts 9:1-19; Galatians 1:11-19;

A. The Truth
B. The Whole Truth
C. Nothing but the Truth

WHO SAYS THAT WHAT GOD SAYS IS TRUE?

Hunting for Truth

Can you remember the game Truth or Dare? We played it as children at parties and overnighters. Most 5th and 6th graders are at an age where Truth or Dare is a favorite party game. The children charge each other to choose either to tell the truth in answer to **any** question, or to have to do something quite out of the ordinary.

At a slumber party attended recently by Abby, my 5th grade daughter, one of the girls was dared to "swim" across the living room floor while singing "Row, Row, Row Your Boat." The truth questions were mostly along the lines of who likes whom.

I wonder what would happen if we played this same game with the adults in our church. Many times in our Christian walk, we are looking for the person who will walk in truth no matter what the cost. Today's Christianity has become a game to many and perhaps some truthful challenges would encourage others to follow Him. We might hear and see some truly amazing things!

As you delve into the subject of God's truth this week, make it a point to share honestly about your own walk with God. Stay away from easy, predictable and religious answers to questions posed. Our 5th and 6th graders need to know that God honors truth above our comfort or ease.

Truth may hurt for a short time, but ultimately it will be the one thing that your students will be able to depend on you for. And remember to always choose truth. It's much easier than the dares.

Materials: Challenge notebooks and Lesson 1 Secret Orders.

♦ Who remembers the main theme of this quarter as we study Galatians? *Grace.*

Let's have a few people share three things they found that Jesus had to say about becoming a Christian.

Have the students place their completed Secret Orders in their Challenge notebooks.

Materials: Paper, pencils, chalkboard and chalk.

We are continuing our study of the book of Galatians today. The subtitle of our study is "Treasure Hunt for Freedom." Today we're going to be exploring truth. Before we begin our lesson, let's go on a treasure hunt to find out what other people believe about truth. In groups of three, take a piece of paper and pencil. You have five minutes to find one person, whether young or old, and ask her this question: "What is truth?" One of you should write down her answer. Find people in the hallway or outside of the classroom.

When the students return to class, have them share the answers they received. Write a synopsis of each answer on the chalkboard. Leave these up throughout today's class, referring to them as you discover different answers to the question from Scripture.

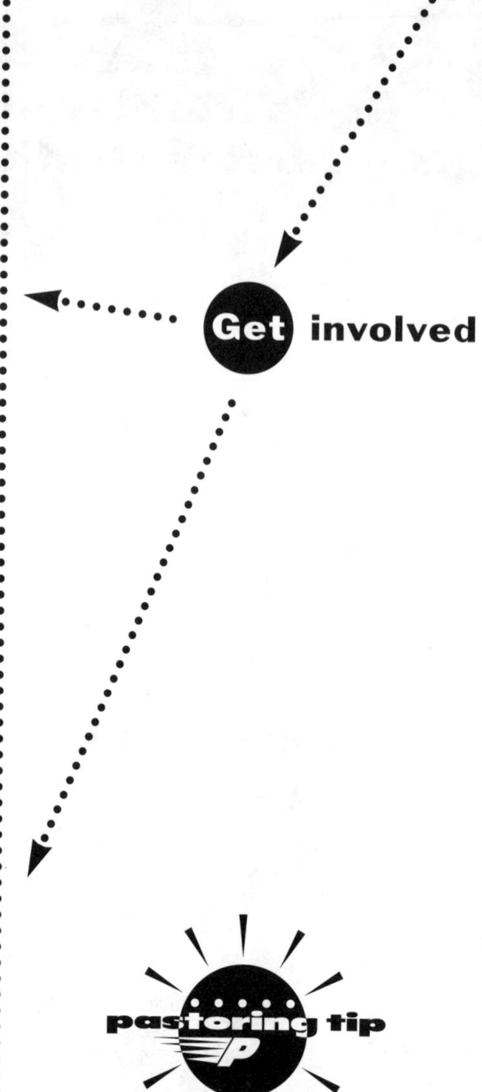

As you prepare to teach this lesson, ask the Holy Spirit for wisdom in touching each student's heart this week.

God's truth is nothing but the truth.

Materials: Bibles, chalkboard, chalk, paper and pencils.

The Truth

Our Power Point today is—*God's truth is nothing but the truth.* Let's take a look at Galatians and discover how Paul found the truth about God and then how he shared that truth. *(Have the students follow along as you read Gal. 1:11-16.)*

♦ **Can you remember how Paul came to know Jesus Christ?** *(Review Acts 9:1-19.)*

Here in Galatians, Paul is telling a little about his life before encountering the truth of who Jesus Christ is.

♦ **What does Paul say he did previously?** *Hurt the church of God very much; tried to destroy the church; did better than most other Jews his age in the Jewish religion; tried harder than anyone else to follow the old rules.*

When he encountered Christ, all of that changed. He began to share the very message he had been fighting against. What he had thought was truth was actually **against** the truth.

Let's read Galatians 1:16-19.

♦ **Who revealed truth to Paul?** *God did.*

After he received the truth, he went to Peter. Peter was the lead elder/pastor for the new church that had started at Pentecost. Paul went to get to know Peter and share what God had shown him. Next week in Galatians 2, we will read that he later went up and told the apostles all that God had said to him. He submitted it to them to be sure he wasn't teaching things that weren't true. Paul wanted to tell the truth and nothing but the truth.

The Whole Truth

There are many ways God reveals truth to us.

♦ **What are some of those?** *Through the Bible, other Christians, pastors, Club 56 leaders, parents, etc.*

(Write this sentence on the chalkboard: Dmvc 67 jt b gvo qmbdf up cf.) **Can anyone decipher this code and tell me what this sentence really says?** The only clue I will give is that the 67 is really a 56. The first person to come up with the answer should write a short sentence in code for the rest of the class. *(The code is that every letter is the letter immediately following the correct letter in the alphabet, so "b" stands for "a," etc.)*

Good job on breaking the code! In God's Word, the Bible, the truth is **not** encoded. It is plain and simple.

Let's look in the Bible right now and find some of that simple truth that might help us in our lives. As I read these verses, someone look them up.

Answer:

Club 56 is a fun place to be.

◊ Matthew 6:31-33—God will take care of us as we put our minds and hearts on Him and His kingdom.

◊ Isaiah 40:31—When we trust the Lord, He will give us strength.

◊ John 1:32-33—Jesus will baptize us in His Spirit.

(As each student reads her Scripture reference, have the others identify what truth is in the passage. Ideas are next to the verses above.)

♦ **How many of you read the Bible sometimes? often? every day?**

The Bible is full of truth. God has given us His Word so we can discover truth from Him. I recommend you read it as often as possible. You'll get lots of truth that will help you in your lives.

Nothing but the Truth

Look at John 14:16-17 and 26. *(Have someone read these verses.)* Jesus called the Holy Spirit "the Spirit of truth." This is because two of His jobs are to teach us and remind us of the things Jesus has said. So, how does the Holy Spirit teach you? Jesus told us that after He went back to heaven, God would send the Holy Spirit to live inside us. He is the part of God that lives in each of us who have received Jesus Christ.

If you have been baptized in the Holy Spirit, He has come alive in you in a new way, has given you gifts and will comfort you. He will speak to you just like He talked to Paul. Let's practice right now listening to Him talk to us. Put your papers and Bibles aside, and I'm going to ask Him to talk to each one of you and to me. God, please come by Your Holy Spirit and speak to us right now. We want to hear Your truth from Your Spirit. Amen.

Now, keep your eyes closed and just listen. *(Stay quiet for one to two minutes.)*

♦ **What did God say to you?** *(Have each student share. Share yourself what God spoke to you.)*

Think of a time in your week when you can get alone with God and listen for Him to tell you His truth for your life. He will give you direction, help in a difficult situation and comfort when things aren't going well.

♦ **How many of you will commit to listen to the Spirit this week?**

Conclusion

In his letter to the Galatians, Paul told them that the truth he had was from God. That same truth-telling is available to all of us today through God's Holy Spirit...the same Spirit that told Paul the truth. All we have to do is listen to Him. We can read God's Word, the Bible, and we can spend time listening to His Holy Spirit. Let's ask Him right now to help us do those two things this week.

Father, we want to be people who understand that Your truth is nothing but the truth. Lord, it's the only truth that matters here on earth. Help us this week to read Your Word and listen to Your Spirit so we know what You are saying and understand Your truth. We love You, God! In Jesus' name, amen.

God's truth is nothing but the truth.

Galatians 1:1 1-12

Brothers, I want you to know that the Good News I preached to you was not made by men. I did not get it from men, nor did any man teach it to me. Jesus Christ showed it to me.

Make the discovery of truth fun for your students.

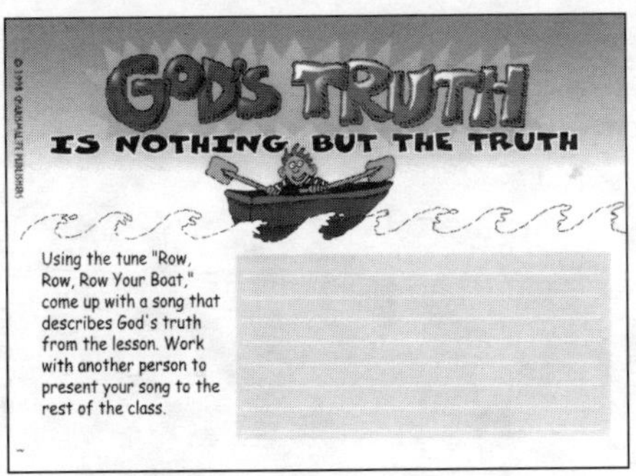

Activity Zone page 3

Materials: Slips of paper, pencils and Bibles.

Today we discussed that the Holy Spirit is truth and He always leads us into truth.

♦ How can we know if what we hear is the truth? *Measure it by the Bible.*

Unless we know what the Bible says, we can be easily fooled by things that sound good or sound right but actually are not what God says.

We are going to play a game that will help us to see how easily we can be fooled by things that sound right. I am going to give you a topic. You are to make up a verse about the topic that sounds like it might come from the Bible. I will write down a real verse from the Bible. Then, I will collect all the verses and mix them up. I will read all the verses to you and you will vote for the verse that you think is the true Bible verse. If the verse you wrote fools anyone, you will receive one point for each person you fool. Let's see how many points each of you can earn.

Give the students the topics listed below. You can use the verses given or choose your own topics and verses. Collect the verses, read them aloud and have the students vote on the verse they think is true. Have the students keep track of their own points.

◊ Pride—Pride leads to arguments, Proverbs 13:10.

◊ Hope—Always be ready to answer everyone who asks you to explain about the hope you have, 1 Peter 3:15b.

◊ Truth—Truth will last forever, but lies last only a moment, Proverbs 12:19.

◊ Holy Spirit—But when the Spirit of truth comes he will lead you into all truth, John 16:13.

1—Music

Materials: Club 56 Activity Zone page 3 and pencils.

What's our Power Point today? *God's truth is nothing but the truth.* We've learned that God has told us the truth in the Bible and that the Holy Spirit speaks the truth to us from Scripture in our hearts and through others. Now we're going to make up a tune to help us remember something we've learned about His truth.

How many of you know the song, "Row, Row, Row Your Boat"? Sing it with students to make sure everyone knows it. On your activity page, write some of the things you've learned about truth today in the space provided. Then work on making them into a song that will fit with the tune of "Row, Row, Row Your Boat." Try to make the song rhyme, but remember the most important part of this activity is to write a song that will help you remember things about God's truth.

2—Bible Study

Materials: *Club 56 Activity Zone* page 4, Bibles, concordances and pencils.

We've been talking about God's truth today. Let's study a little more about it from another book of the Bible. Use the concordances to look up verses about "truth" in the book of Psalms. Pick out one of those verses and answer the questions on your activity page.

Have students share their answers with the whole group.

3—Group Art

Materials: Chalkboard, chalk, posterboard, markers, scissors, glue and construction paper.

Before class: Write "God said it. I believe it. That settles it." on the chalkboard. Cut the pieces of posterboard into four strips horizontally so there is one strip for each student.

Show the saying on the board. **There's a bumper sticker that says this: "God said it. I believe it. That settles it." It's a brief way of saying some of the same things we learned in our lesson today.**

Each of you can now make that statement in a variety of ways. Using the supplies, make this saying on your piece of posterboard. You can cut out letters from the construction paper, write balloon letters and decorate them with markers or use a combination of those two things.

Be as creative as you can, but remember, the point is for you to remember the saying and that God's truth is all we need to believe in.

Have students share their posters with the class.

4—Cooking

Materials: Popcorn (popped, one gallon), brown sugar (2 cups), margarine (1 cup), corn syrup (1/2 cup), salt (1 teaspoon), can of peanuts (small), pot (large), hot plate, wooden spoon, paper bag (large), cookie sheet, plastic bags (small), slips of paper, pens, aluminum foil and Bibles.

Before class: Pop one gallon of popcorn and put it into a large paper bag. This will yield approximately 12 small bags of caramel corn.

People are always searching for something better they think will make them happier.

Activity Zone page 4

Most kids will need help using a concordance. Show them how to use it in small groups, assigning children who catch on quickly to continue explaining to those who didn't understand.

God's truth is nothing but the truth.

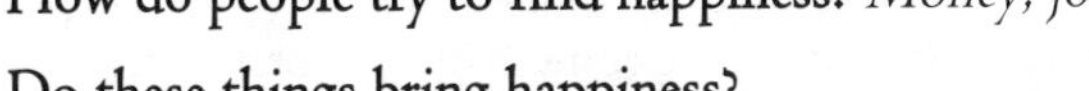

♦ How do people try to find happiness? *Money, jobs, things.*

♦ Do these things bring happiness?

What people want is to know the truth about the meaning of life. When we have a relationship with Jesus, we don't have to search. We know where to find the truth...in the Bible. As our Power Point tells us—*God's truth is nothing but the truth!*

We are going to make something we can give to others that can help them find the truth.

♦ Have you ever had Cracker Jack popcorn?

♦ What is your favorite part? Wait until someone says "the prize."

When you have a box of Cracker Jack popcorn, don't you always go searching to find the prize? Well, we are going to make caramel corn that has a prize. But this time, instead of finding tattoos or riddles, the person searching for the prize will find real truth from the Bible.

The students can make the caramel corn by taking turns making the following recipe:

1. Melt the following in a large pan on a hot plate: 1 cup margarine, 2 cups brown sugar, 1/2 cup corn syrup and 1 teaspoon salt. Boil for 5 minutes, stirring frequently. Add a small can of peanuts.

2. Pour the caramel over the popcorn in the paper bag. Then have students take turns shaking the popcorn in the bag until it is well coated.

3. Spread it out on a cookie sheet and let it dry.

While the caramel corn is drying, ask the students to use their Bibles to find a few verses they would like to use as the prizes in the snacks. Help them use a concordance to find the verses they desire. After they have written them on small pieces of paper, they should fold them in aluminum foil and place the foil prizes in the small plastic bags. Then add the caramel corn to the bags. The students can take home the snacks and share them with others.

Your 5th and 6th graders need to feel valued. Listen carefully when they answer a question, whether or not you agree with their answers.

Materials: Copies of Living It Out story.

Hi, I'm Carolyn Ann. We have to talk! I am so worried, and I'm kind of uncomfortable talking to the kids who are in Club 56 with me. You know, I just don't want anyone to think I'm getting strange or anything. Let me tell you what happened, and then maybe you can tell me what you would have done. I just have a funny feeling that this could happen again.

Well, we were all in Club 56 today and the teacher asked us to pray for each other. That seems pretty easy, huh? I was doing what she asked us to do. In fact, I was praying in my special prayer language when all of a sudden I had this really strong thought that I was to pray for my friend, Maxi, because God was preparing her to be a missionary. Whoa! Where did that come from? I opened my eyes to see if anything unusual was going on in the room, but everyone looked just like they always do. I couldn't concentrate then because I wasn't sure what I should do about what I thought God said.

Maybe I ought to tell you a little more. See, Maxi is my best friend, and I know that she really cares about the people in South America. Her mom is from Brazil. So maybe I just thought this up because I know that she would like to go there someday? What do you think? Could I just be thinking this up in my own head? I don't want to do something that might make Maxi change her life and then find out I'm wrong! But I want to do what God wants me to do, too. I've been asking Him to show me how to serve Him better.

Now here's something I need to know: Are you supposed to tell people that you think God is saying something to them? Or maybe you're just supposed to pray for them. I wonder if I should talk to my Sunday School teacher?

You know, this is pretty important information. Shouldn't God tell adults things like this instead of kids? What would you do if this happened to you? Has it ever happened to you? Well, if you could talk about this and get back to me, I would really appreciate it. I want to do the right thing. Thanks.

How would you answer Carolyn?

Divide the class into small discussion groups. Give each group a copy of the Living It Out story. Ask each group to make a list of Carolyn's questions and see how they would answer them on the basis of today's lesson. When the small groups have completed their discussions, ask them to share their thoughts.

Materials: Copies of Lesson 2 Secret Orders.

OK. I'm hearing that you did a pretty good job last week on the assignment I gave you. Do I know how to pick them or what?

This week we are looking at the truth. Everybody wants to tell their version of what they say is true. It can be a tough job getting at the real truth. Sometimes we are forced to use a lie detector or a dose of truth serum just to verify what people try to tell us. That's why the Bible is so great. It really is the whole truth and nothing but the truth.

Your assignment is to write out your definition of truth, how important truth is to you, how you feel about lying and in what circumstance you might not tell the truth. Be honest.

Remember to bring your completed Secret Orders to class next week.

Find time each week to encourage individual students to listen to God's voice.

God's truth is nothing but the truth.

SECRET ORDERS

ITEMS NEEDED FOR LESSON

❑ Challenge notebooks
❑ Lesson 2 Secret Orders

1—Drama

❑ *Club 56 Activity Zone* page 5
❑ Pencils

2—Outreach Project

❑ Paper
❑ Pencil

❑ Chalkboard
❑ Chalk
❑ Paper
❑ Pencils

3—Game

❑ *Club 56 Activity Zone* page 6
❑ Pencils

❑ Bibles
❑ Chalkboard
❑ Chalk

4—Problem Solving

❑ Styrofoam cups (50)

❑ Chalkboard
❑ Chalk
❑ Bubble gum (two pieces per student)
❑ Toothpicks
❑ Index cards
❑ Antibacterial soap
❑ Water
❑ Paper towel

❑ None

❑ Copies of Lesson 3 Secret Orders

SPECIAL NOTE

This week's lesson is about the team concept. Your students are very aware of team activities in sports, entertainment, politics and education. Help them see that each person in the body of Christ plays an important role on the team God has assembled as His family.

The team concept: Created by God.

When we have the opportunity to help anyone, we should do it. But we should give special attention to those who are in the family of believers.
Galatians 6:10

Galatians 2:1-2,8-10; 5:1,13-14; Ephesians 6:12

A. The Team

B. The Coach

C. The Game

3

THE GOD TEAM

Hunting for God's Team

I can think of several different teams I've been on in the past 25 years. Each team had different goals, but all the teams had the same overarching goal: to win the game we were playing.

There was the women's basketball team I played on while doing a one-year missionary tour in South Korea. We practiced a lot and really only played one game—against the junior high boys team to "help them work out." Guess who got the workout?

Another team I played on was a coed church volleyball team. The team was great fun. There was a lot of competition during the games and good fellowship afterwards when we all went together to get some sodas.

I've been on several staff teams at different churches—people whom God had called together to do His work in a particular body of believers. Some of those teams have been excellent, with everyone working together for the common good. Some of those teams, though, were difficult due to our immaturity, jealousy or desire for position.

The team about which you will begin sharing with your students today is so much bigger than any of these teams. It's the team of people around the globe who have chosen to follow God and do what He says. It includes all the other Club 56 leaders around the United States. It includes your students. It includes pastors, mothers and members of congress. It includes people we might not even agree with theologically, but who nonetheless make up a distinct part of His team.

Before teaching this lesson, sit down with God and let Him encourage you by showing you all the people on our team. We are truly blessed by Him to have a team to achieve the goals of His kingdom.

Materials: Challenge notebooks and Lesson 2 Secret Orders.

Last week we answered several questions about truth. Let's have some of you share your answers.

♦ What is your definition of truth?

♦ How important is truth to you?

♦ How do you feel about lying?

♦ What about any circumstances when you might not tell the truth?

Have the students place their completed Secret Orders in their Challenge notebooks.

Materials: Chalkboard, chalk, paper and pencils.

Before class: Write the Power Point on the chalkboard.

We're continuing our study of Galatians today. Who remembers the subtitle of Galatians? *Treasure Hunt for Freedom.* **Let's begin today's lesson by having you get into teams and hunt for some words in our Power Point. I've written the Power Point on the board. Read it with me.** Have the whole class say the Power Point together. Break the class into teams of three students. Only one team member will need to write down the team's words.

You and your team will have four minutes to find as many words as you can using the letters from our Power Point. For instance, you might find the word "cone." You can take letters out of order, but you can only use letters that appear in the Power Point. At the end of four minutes, we'll compare everyone's lists and see who came up with the most words.

Have the students tell the words they found.

You did really well working as teams and hunting for the words. Let's begin our Bible lesson.

The team concept: Created by God.

Keep the team concept going from week to week so your students understand they are part of something much bigger than just your class or church.

Materials: Bibles, chalkboard and chalk.

The Team

♦ **What book of the Bible are we studying?** *Galatians.*

♦ **Who wrote it?** *Paul.*

♦ **What are the Power Points from the last two weeks?** *Discover God by knowing Jesus. God's truth is nothing but the truth.*

You are doing really well learning about the book of Galatians. This week and next we will be looking at teamwork. Our Power Point today is—**The team concept: Created by God.** Listen as I read some verses from the second chapter of Galatians and see if you can hear who was on Paul's team. *(Read Gal. 2:1-2,8-10.) Barnabas, Titus, James, Peter and John.*

Now look in your own Bibles and, using the verses I just read, find out how the two teams were different. *Barnabas, Titus and Paul and were called to tell the Good News to the people who weren't Jews. James, Peter and John were all called to tell the Good News to the Jews.*

Each of the people mentioned had a part, but all of them together made a team.

♦ **Can you deduce, then, who's on our team? Who works with us the same way these people worked with Paul?** *Your pastor, the ushers, nursery workers, evangelists, Billy Graham, other Christians in your town from different churches, etc.*

♦ **What happens if any of these team members don't play?** *The team isn't complete, so we won't be able to achieve our goals as well as we could with our whole team together.*

Just as Paul and his teammates worked together to tell others about Jesus, so we are called to work with many different people, both young and old, to follow our Coach and win the game. That brings us to two good questions: who's the Coach and what's the game?

The Coach

So, if they were all on the same team, who was the Coach? Paul? Peter? James? No, the Coach of the team they were on is God. He is actually the owner and the Coach of the team. He calls the shots. He's the One who revealed His truth to Paul and told him to go to the non-Jewish people. He's also the One who told James, Peter and John to preach the Good News to the Jews. God knew what each member of the team needed to do.

God's our coach, too. We have a team here at our church.

♦ **What is the purpose of our team?**

- Whom are we opposing?
- Who do you think will win?

The Game

So we know who's on our team and we know who our Coach is, but some of you might be wondering what the game is. Let's do a Scripture hunt and see if we can find out some things about the "game" we're playing.

Put your Bibles on your laps. Fold your hands on top of your Bibles. I will call out a Scripture, and when I say go, you can pick up your Bible and look for the verse. When you find it, stand up with your finger at that place in the Bible. The person who finds it first will read it. When that person has finished, if you can tell what it says about the game we're in, raise your hand. The first person to stand will give his answer. *(Use the following verses in the game, talking about each one after the students find it.)*

◊ Ephesians 6:12—Our fight is against the spiritual powers of evil.

◊ Galatians 5:1—We're standing for freedom in Christ.

◊ Galatians 5:13-14—We're working to love other people.

In reality, none of these are games. They are very serious things we face as Christians. God gave us a team to work with as we face them. He is our Coach. He's helping us, giving us wisdom and truth to do the right things when we face Satan, when we stand up for freedom in Christ and when we love other people.

Conclusion

There's a saying using the letters of *team* as an acrostic. *(Write TEAM vertically on the chalkboard, writing this saying after each letter.)*

◊ Together

◊ Everyone

◊ Accomplishes

◊ More

This saying reminds us that we're not on God's team all by ourselves. We need our Coach, God, and the other players, Christians both young and old. When everyone is working together, we can accomplish what God has sent us here to earth to accomplish. Let's pray right now that the Lord will help us this week to work together with other Christians to see His kingdom expanded here on earth.

Father, please help us this week to listen to You, our Coach. Help each of us to obey the things You ask us to do. As we work together on things, both here in Club 56 and each day during the week, help us to accomplish Your goals—to win the game You've called us to play. Thank You, God. In Jesus' name, amen.

The team concept: Created by God.

Find time to personally tell each student he is on your team.

Galatians 6:10

When we have the opportunity to help anyone, we should do it. But we should give special attention to those who are in the family of believers.

Materials: Chalkboard, chalk, bubble gum (two pieces per student), toothpicks, index cards, antibacterial soap, water and paper towels.

Before class: Write the Memory Verse on the chalkboard.

Today we've talked about God's team, which consists of us, our Coach and other people who believe in Him.

♦ **What different kinds of teams can you think of?** *Soccer, cooperative learning teams, basketball, baseball, etc.*

On God's team, we are all star players. He's the coach and we each listen to Him and do what He tells us to. **Let's learn our Memory Verse this morning by reading it together.** Read it together several times, then let students say it by themselves without looking at the board.

Now that you know it well, we're going to make sculptures that represent something in the verse. You will make your sculpture out of bubble gum and toothpicks on these index cards. You must first chew the bubble gum, then take it out and shape it using your fingers or toothpicks to do so.

When the sculptures are done, have the students share them and tell what they represent from the verse.

1—Drama

Materials: *Club 56 Activity Zone* page 5 and pencils.

Pass out the activity page. **Read the instructions on the page and work with a group of three or four to plan and portray the skits.**

Give groups five minutes to talk about and prepare their skits. Have each group show their skit to the class. Have the class answer these questions after each group has finished.

♦ How did the characters work together?

♦ What groups could we help in our own neighborhood, church or schools?

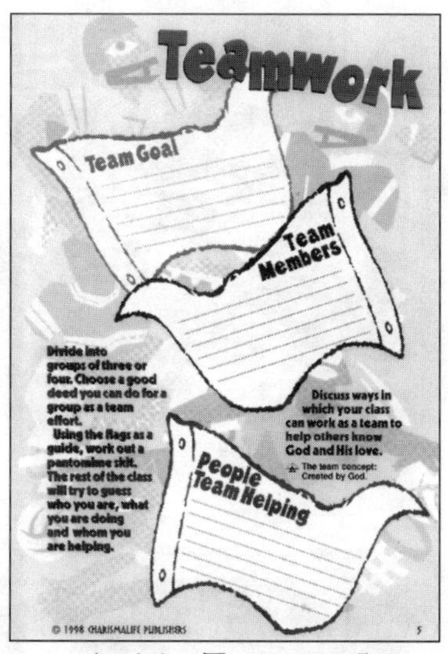

Activity Zone page 5

2—Outreach Project

Materials: Paper and pencils.

Before class: Contact your pastor or children's pastor and find some projects you and your class can help with around the church. Suggestions are: cleaning, organizing cupboards, landscaping, washing windows, etc. It will be best if you have a list from which the class can choose. You will need supplies for the various activities ready or in a place where they are easily accessible.

♦ **What is our Power Point today?** *The team concept: Created by God.*

We are a part of a larger team here in our church. The team is made up of every person who loves God and is a member of our church.

♦ **What are some things our team does?** *Tell other people about the Lord; have worship services; provide kids' ministry; care for babies during the service, etc.*

Some things you may never think about that must be done by members of our team are cleaning this building, washing windows, taking the trash out, etc. For our Outreach Project this week, we're going to participate on our team in a different way. Right now we will take a look at this list of things that needs to be done and choose one or two in which we can all participate.

Have students choose activities they can do during class time. Suggest another day or time when the entire class can be together and do some of the other activities.

3—Game

Materials: *Club 56 Activity Zone* page 6 and pencils.

In our lesson today, our Power Point emphasizes the importance of Christians working together as a team. God did not intend for His followers to go through life alone. He knows we need the support, encouragement and help of others.

♦ How can a team help you when you have a problem? a difficult job to do?

We are going to play a game that emphasizes the importance and benefits of working together as a team. You will be divided into two groups and will be given a task. Your group will have to figure out the fastest way to correctly complete the job. The team finishing the activity first is the winner.

Hand out the activity pages and pencils. Give each student a number. The students with even numbers are on one team and the students with odd numbers are on the second team. Without giving advice, have the students complete the activity. Then, discuss the following questions:

♦ How did your team decide to complete the game?

♦ Do you think you could have answered all the questions on your own?

♦ How did being part of a team help?

In the game, we found that the better we worked as teams, the more successful we were. The same is true in our lives. God knows we need each other. As our Power Point tells us, the team concept was created by Him!

If the cleaning sounds uninteresting to some of your students, add a little competition by breaking them into teams and giving points for different kinds of jobs.

When doing a competitive activity, be sure to encourage both winning and losing teams.

Activity Zone page 6

The team concept: Created by God.

4—Problem Solving

Materials: Styrofoam cups (50).

I am going to give each of you some Styrofoam cups. I want you to decide on a way to stack them as high as you can without damaging them. Hand out the cups and give them a few minutes to build their towers. Those look pretty good, but they are really not that high. Now I want you to join with two or three other people and build your towers again. Combine your ideas and cups and see how high you can make your tower. Again give them a few minutes to complete their towers.

Those look great! Now let's see how high we can make our towers when we combine all of our resources and ideas. Let your students build their giant tower using all the cups and the best ideas reflected in the past towers. See how great our tower is when we work together, combine our ideas and resources! The family of God is the same way. When we realize God has placed us together with our different gifts and abilities, we can reach out to those around us with a unified strength. Together is better in reaching our world for Christ.

I'm Paul Decker, and I am really mad. Have you ever had a really good idea and people walked all over it? Well, that just happened to me.

In Club 56 our leader, Mr. Jenkins, asked us to come up with some ideas for a club newspaper. I think it should have been obvious to him that I would be the best editor. I know the most about newspapers because my dad owns the biggest newspaper in town! That counts for something, doesn't it? Apparently not, because when I suggested it, Mr. Jenkins said that wasn't what he had in mind.

Mr. Jenkins said instead of having one editor, we are going to run the paper as a team. We'll all work together and make group decisions. That doesn't even make sense to me. Do you know who he put on the editorial team? No, I didn't think you would. Kyle! Dumb-as-dirt Kyle! He doesn't know a poem from a pig. It looks to me like I might as well bail on this whole paper thing.

My dad said I have a bad attitude and I need to pray. Now that's a typical parent remark. But what really made me mad was when Todd, my best friend, told me I was acting like a jerk. He said I think I'm the lone ranger! I don't want anyone else to know this, but that really hurt my feelings. After all the things I've done for him.

I think I'm just going to call Mr. Jenkins tomorrow and tell him his little plan stinks. He needs to find the best, most qualified people to do things and let them get at it. That makes sense to me. He told us in class that we could learn from each other. Right! What in the world could I ever learn from Kyle?

I'm sure you see what I'm saying, don't you? Why don't you talk about this and see what you think? After all, this could happen to you sometime, this whole team business, I mean. Let me know, OK?

How can you encourage Paul?

Divide the class into small groups and have them discuss the questions below. After their discussions, assign each group a position (Mr. Jenkins' or Paul's) on this subject and ask them to prepare a defense to present to the class.

♦ Why would Paul's best friend, Todd, tell Paul that he thinks he's the lone ranger?

♦ What seems to be Mr. Jenkins' purpose in using an editorial team rather than one editor?

Using your Bible lesson for today, give Paul scriptural reasons why working as a team is good.

♦ What do you think is the greatest challenge about working with a group of people, even Christians?

♦ What makes working with a group of people interesting?

♦ How could Paul help Kyle rather than judge him so harshly?

(Materials:) Copies of Lesson 3 Secret Orders.

All this investigating can get to be quite a drag. That's why on most stake-outs we like to team up with a partner. It helps to have someone there with you to back you up so you don't have to go it completely alone.

Your assignment this week should be a breeze. Think about three of your closest friends—don't worry, I don't want you to rat on them or anything like that. I want you to come up with some of the important things you have in common. Then explain why that helps you to be great friends.

Remember to bring your completed Secret Orders to class next week.

Include children on your "team" by asking them to pray for you, your family or a friend of yours.

The team concept: Created by God.

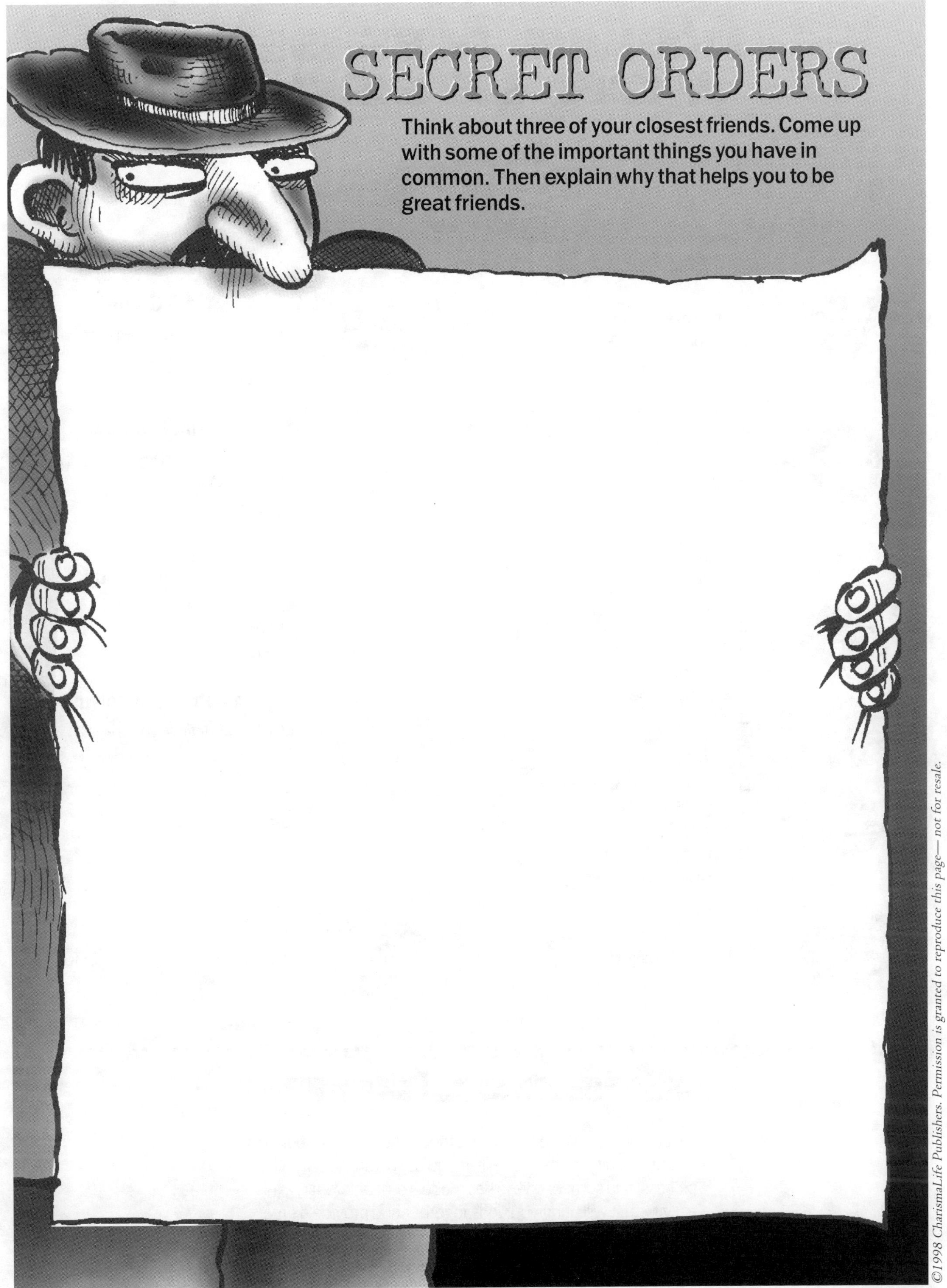

SECRET ORDERS

Think about three of your closest friends. Come up with some of the important things you have in common. Then explain why that helps you to be great friends.

ITEMS NEEDED FOR LESSON

❑ Challenge notebooks
❑ Lesson 3 Secret Orders

1—Game

❑ *Club 56 Activity Zone* page 7
❑ Pencils
❑ Prize

❑ Paper
❑ Pencils

2—Individual Art

❑ Marshmallows (large, small)
❑ Toothpicks
❑ Pens
❑ Paper

❑ Bibles
❑ Chalkboard
❑ Chalk
❑ Paper
❑ Pencils
❑ M&M's
❑ Knitting needles
❑ Yarn

3—Bible Study

❑ Bibles
❑ Pencils
❑ Paper

4—Problem Solving

❑ *Club 56 Activity Zone* page 8
❑ Posterboard
❑ Tape
❑ Marker
❑ Pencils

❑ Fabric (various, 120, 6-inch squares)
❑ Fabric (5- by 6-foot piece)
❑ Cotton batting (5- by 6-foot)
❑ Thread (quilting)
❑ Fabric pens (or fabric paints)
❑ Plastic sheet (or newspapers)

❑ Copies of Living It Out story

❑ Copies of Lesson 4 Secret Orders

SPECIAL NOTE

For our Memory Verse activity this week you are going to have an opportunity to make a quilt. If you are unfamiliar with the process, find someone who has made a quilt before. It is a fun activity that will bring your kids together and provide a great outreach opportunity.

It's what we have in common that counts.

Help each other with your troubles. When you do this, you truly obey the law of Christ. If anyone thinks that he is important when he is really not important, he is only fooling himself.

Galatians 6:2-3

Galatians 3:26-29; 5:4-5; 6:1-5

A. It's Common Knowledge

B. A Knitting Lesson

C. Compared to Her...

ONLY ONE STAR PLAYER ON THIS TEAM: GOD!

When I think about you, another Club 56 teacher, I often have this thought: your class is better than mine. Isn't that silly? I don't even know most of you! In my mind, though, you spend at least six hours a week preparing for class, have every activity ready and waiting for the kids, call each child every week, have the perfect classroom setting, handle every situation with ease and present your lesson in such a way that every kid walks away changed. I'm just sure you have your act together in the many areas I don't.

I've worked in children's ministries long enough to know the truth, though. You and I are very much the same. Many times our lessons get thrown together on Saturday evening or early Sunday morning. We intended to call at least one student this week, but our own families and schedules filled the time. The supplies we needed for activities are unavailable since we planned so late, so once again we'll be doing one of those great Club 56 activities, only in a make-shift way. Our classroom is missing some key ingredient, and we all have at least one student who strengthens our prayer life.

I compare myself so easily with others "out there." The lesson today brings me again to our Father. I want to again remember the things I have in common with each of you as we prepare this week for the kids God will bring to us. Like me, you are loved by God. Like you, I am His child through Jesus Christ. Whether we are rich or poor, male or female, or black-, brown- or white-skinned, God has called all of us to be in His body together and to minister to a same-aged group of kids. I'm excited to be working with you this week to further God's kingdom. Remember, *It's what we have in common that counts!*

Materials: Challenge notebooks and Lesson 3 Secret Orders.

Review last week's challenge and have your students share what they have in common with their friends and why that helps them to be good friends.

Have the students place their completed Secret Orders in their Challenge notebooks.

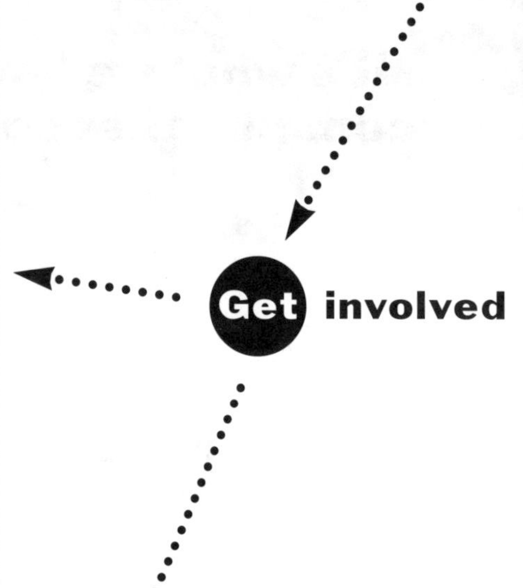

Materials: Paper and pencils.

Let's play a game to help us begin to think about our Power Point today. Everyone needs a piece of paper. Your mission is to get to each person in the classroom in the next five minutes and find three things that are similar between you and the other person. It might be that you have the same number of kids in your family, or that your parents have similar jobs or that you both like watching tennis on television. You must write one or two words next to each name that will help you to remember what you have in common with that person. Ready? Go.

Play this game with the class yourself. At the end, have the students share one or two things each that they have in common with someone that they didn't know when they began the game.

Our Power Point today is—*It's what we have in common that counts.* Let's get right into our Bible Lesson.

It's what we have in common that counts.

Materials: Bibles, chalkboard, chalk, paper, pencils, M&Ms, knitting needles and yarn.

Before class: If you are unfamiliar with knitting, have a church member who knits come to show the students how a single strand of yarn becomes a piece of knitting.

It's Common Knowledge

♦ **What was our Power Point last week?** *The team concept: Created by God.*

♦ **Can you remember who was on Paul's team?** *Barnabas, Titus, James, Peter and John.*

♦ **How were the two teams different that Paul was on?** *Barnabas and Titus traveled with him to tell the non-Jews about Jesus; James, Peter and John told the Jews about Jesus.*

This week we're going to expand a little on the team concept. Our Power Point this week is—**It's what we have in common that counts.** As we read this next passage, count how many things Paul writes that we have in common with other believers. *(Have the students read Gal. 3:26-29.)* There are five different things: We are baptized into Christ. We are clothed with Christ. We are children of God. We are all the same in Christ. We belong to Christ and we get all of the blessings of God.

Paul is telling the people they had a lot of things in common. In verse 28, he tells them three things they might think make them different from other Christians. Let's list those things on the chalkboard.

◊ If they were Jews or Greeks

◊ If they were slaves or free men

◊ If they were male or female

♦ **Which of those three things still divide people in the church today?** *(Allow students to share their opinions.)*

♦ **If you know a 5th or 6th grader who lets one of those things make her feel different from others in the church, how might verses 28-29 help you correct that wrong thinking?**

Paul is telling the people that it's what we have in common that counts, not what is different. We all belong to Christ. We are God's children. We have been saved by the blood of Jesus. All these things and many others make us more similar to each other than we are different from each other.

Let's see how well you do at a little game about similarities and differences. In groups of two, list as many things as you can that you both have in common with the president of the United States. Then make a list of things you do not have in common with him. The team that comes up with the most original answers (that is, no other teams have the same answers on their papers) will win a prize. *(Allow one minute for the contest. Have one group at a time read their list. All groups should cross off anything that is the same on their lists. One point should be given for each common thing that did not show up on any other group's list. Award the group with the most points five M&M's apiece.)*

A Knitting Lesson

God wants to knit us together with other people who belong to Him. *(Begin the demonstration of knitting.)* When a knitter begins a project all she has is a skein of yarn and two knitting needles. You might look at it and wonder how this could become a sweater or some other article. The knitter takes time to make the right stitches, keeps just the right tension on the yarn, and follows the directions in order for a perfect project to come out. God is the same way. He "knits" us together in His love. Let's look at some of the ways He does that. Look at Galatians 6:1-5. Read it yourself and tell me two ways God might use to knit you together with someone else who loves Him. (There are several ways listed.) *Help someone who has done something wrong to make it right. Be careful when helping someone because you might be tempted to something wrong also. Help each other with troubles. Don't compare yourself with others. Be responsible for yourself.*

Wow! God is expecting us to work together in the church. This isn't just for adults, either! This applies right here in our Club 56 meetings.

♦ **How might you help someone in our class who has done something wrong?**

♦ **How could you help someone who is having troubles?**

♦ **What does it mean to be responsible for yourself?**

God wants to knit us together. He wants all of us here to work with each other as a team to do His work. Let's pray right now that He will help us to do that.

Father God, please help us in Club 56 to be a team. Lord, help us to remember what we have in common rather than what divides us. Help us to truly help each other, Lord. If we start comparing ourselves to others in this class, please stop us in our minds and remind us that we don't need to compare; we need to follow and listen to You. We love You, Lord. In Jesus' name, amen.

Compared to Her...

Look at Galatians 5:4-5. *(Read these verses out loud.)*

♦ **To whom have you ever compared yourself?** *(Allow students to respond.)*

It's pretty easy to look at someone and think you're better or worse than she is in some way. We do it all the time. You've probably already done it in some ways this morning. Let me list some ways that might happen in Club 56. Don't tell me which specific ones you have thought about, but when I'm done listing them, tell me if you've thought of any of these things in comparison to other students in this class. *(Use the list below, writing it on the chalkboard. Add to it things that you think of with your students.)*

◊ The way someone prays

◊ The clothes someone wears

◊ The things someone talks about

Pray for a breakthrough in your students with each other that comparison would be kept to a minimum so that true ministry can take place in the Spirit.

It's what we have in common that counts.

◊ The answers someone gives

◊ The way someone does her hair

◊ The way someone sings

So, have you ever compared yourself, either negatively or positively, to someone else in our class in one or more of these ways?

Paul is instructing us not to compare ourselves to others.

♦ **What might be some drawbacks of comparing yourself to someone else?**

♦ **What does Paul say to do instead of comparing?** *Judge your own actions only. Be proud of what you've done. Be responsible for yourself only.*

The next time comparison thoughts come into your mind, try doing one of those three things: think about and discuss with God your own actions, pat yourself on the back for good things you've done and take responsibility for your own deeds.

Conclusion

We have lots of wonderful things in common with each other and others in the church. God is helping us to come together by knitting us together in His love. He has given us clear instructions about not comparing ourselves to others. On His team, He wants us to focus on our similarities, not our differences.

Before we finish our lesson, I want you to talk to God and let Him give you a word to give to someone else that will help them see what you have in common, how we can work together as a team or how they can stop comparing. Pray with me.

God, please speak to each of us right now so all of us can be Your team working together. Give us encouraging words to give to each other. Thank You. Amen.

Now, sit quietly and listen to the Holy Spirit's voice. Sometime after class, go to the person He gave you an encouraging word for and tell her what God said to you. Let's be the team God made us to be.

Galatians 6:2-3

Help each other with your troubles. When you do this, you truly obey the law of Christ. If anyone thinks that he is important when he is really not important, he is only fooling himself.

Materials: Fabric (various, 120, 6-inch squares), fabric (5- by 6-foot piece), cotton batting (5- by 6-foot), thread (quilting), fabric pens (or fabric paints) and plastic sheet (or newspapers).

Before class: Find a volunteer in your church who would be willing to sew a simple quilt together for your class. After your students have decorated the quilt squares, you will give them to the volunteer, along with pieces of fabric and batting (each 5- by 6-foot) and thread. You can ask people in the church to donate the materials or you can call a fabric store to ask if they have remnants they would be willing to donate.

This week's Memory Verse encourages us to help others with their troubles. We are told to help each other when we have troubles. Let's begin by taking a few minutes to memorize our verse. After they have memorized the verse and recited it to partners, discuss the following:

♦ What troubles do people have that we could help them with?

♦ How could we help in practical ways?

We can read about a woman in the Bible (Tabitha, or Dorcas), who was well-known and loved for her kindness in helping others (Acts 9:36-43). She was known for sewing for others. Today, we are going to begin sewing a quilt.

♦ How could we use this quilt to help someone?

Give the students time to brainstorm a list of people to whom they could give the quilt. Then allow them to vote as a class for whom they would like to help with their quilt. Discuss ideas for how they might decorate their quilt squares. They could draw pictures of encouragement, hope or love. Or they could draw pictures of ways they could help others. Cover the table with the plastic sheet. Hand out the quilt squares and fabric pens. You may choose to decorate all 80 squares or decorate 40 squares and alternate them on the quilt with plain squares.

After class, give the squares, batting, fabric and thread to your volunteer. When the quilt is finished, show it to the class. If possible, allow a few of the students to deliver the quilt to the person chosen by the class.

1–Game

Materials: *Club 56 Activity Zone* page 7, pencils and prize.

What's our Power Point today? *It's what we have in common that counts.* We've talked about some of the things we have in common when we are Christians. Let's see what else we have in common.

Hand out the activity pages and pencils. **As I read the statement, mark through it on your card if it applies to you. This is a bingo game, so you need to mark all the boxes in a row of five either across, up and down or diagonally.**

Award a prize to the student who says bingo first. Have the students tell who is similar to them in the classroom, using the bingo sheets.

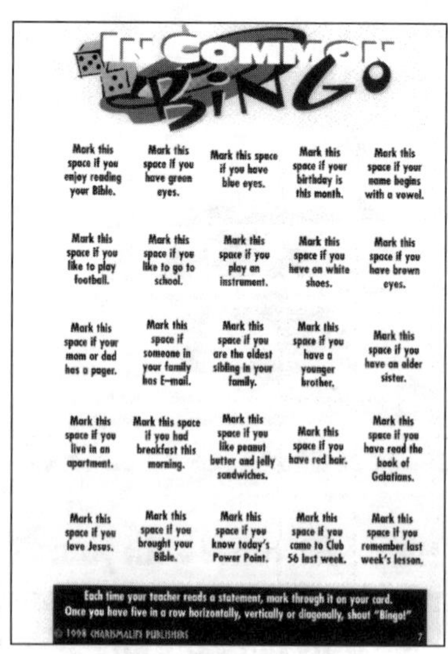

Activity Zone page 7

pastoring tip

Some students shy away from creative projects. Encourage those students by sitting down and talking through a possible creation with them.

Activity Zone page 8

2—Individual Art

Materials: Marshmallows (large, small), toothpicks, pens and paper.

We all make up the same team (God's), but we all have different parts to play on the team. For our art project this morning, we're going to use common materials, marshmallows and toothpicks, to see how very different our thinking is.

Give each student 20 small marshmallows, five large marshmallows, 15 toothpicks and a piece of paper. Using the paper as a mat, have them each make an animal, either real or imagined. Have them write their names on their papers.

When everyone is done, have the students explain their creations. **Everyone's animal is different, but all have several things in common.**

♦ **What do they have in common?** *All have the same number of marshmallows and toothpicks to work with. All of them are animals.*

♦ **Are any of the creations wrong?** *No. The instructions left the kind of creation up to the individual, so none can be wrong.*

3—Bible Study

Materials: Bibles, pencils and paper.

At the beginning of the book of Genesis, there are four characters who all were supposed to be working as teams with God to accomplish His purposes. These people were Adam, Eve, Cain and Abel. Unfortunately, they blew their chances for becoming great teams. Look up their stories in Genesis 1-4 and answer these questions about them. You can choose either the team of Adam and Eve or the team of Cain and Abel to write about.

♦ What did they have in common with each other?

♦ What was different between them?

♦ How could they have used their similarities to help build a team?

♦ How did their differences cause them to tear down the team?

4—Problem Solving

Materials: *Club 56 Activity Zone* page 8, posterboard, tape, marker and pencils.

Before class: Tape the posterboard to the wall.

Today we talked about the importance of loving and serving others. The best example we have of a person who served and helped others was Jesus.

♦ In what ways did Jesus help and serve others?

♦ How can we follow Jesus' example?

♦ In what troubles can we help others? *Financial, death of a loved one, loneliness, sickness, old age, etc.*

As the students come up with troubles, write them down on the posterboard. Then have them choose two or three of the troubles named and come up with as many ways as possible of bearing people's burdens and helping them in practical ways. Remind them that help can come in the form of physical, emotional and spiritual assistance.

Hand out the activity pages and pencils. **Now that we have come up with some ways to help others, I want you to think of someone you can help. Using your activity page, I want you to write her name, the situation in which she needs help and five practical ways in which you can serve her.**

Encourage the students to think of someone specific in their own lives whom they could help by serving.

After the students have completed the activity, ask for volunteers to share with the class. Encourage your students to follow through this week by serving the person they wrote about.

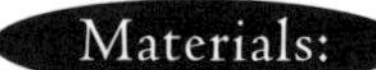 Materials: Copies of Living It Out questions.

Heidi listened with growing frustration as her partner on the Club 56 Gazette interviewed the pastor. This just wasn't going the way she had planned. "Uhm, so uhm, do you like being a priest?" Carol Ann asked haltingly.

"He's not a priest, Carol Ann," interrupted Heidi urgently. "He's a pastor!"

Carol Ann looked confused and blinked back tears. "You're doing just great, Carol Ann," said Pastor Hicks kindly. "Keep going."

Oh great, thought Heidi, *now I look like a jerk. I will demand a new partner before this day is over!*

The Club 56 editorial team had made the reporter assignments and she had a feeling that Todd, her brother, and his friend Paul had deliberately put her with Carol Ann. They knew that she didn't think Carol Ann should even be a reporter. She was new to the church, and what did they really know about her anyway?

Later that day Heidi talked to Mr. Jenkins to see if she could get a different partner, someone like her good friend Janae. "You know, Heidi," he smiled kindly, "you could be a wonderful new friend to Carol Ann. This could be an opportunity to share the love of Jesus." For a minute she thought she had wandered into "Mr. Rogers' Neighborhood!"

"Mr. Jenkins, I hardly know Carol Ann, and she doesn't seem to be like the kids I usually do things with..." The rest of Heidi's words seemed to trail off. The look on Mr. Jenkins face made Heidi uncomfortable. He seemed sad and the last thing she wanted to do was leave a bad impression. She quickly decided that she would have to find another way to change partners. "You know what, Mr. Jenkins? Everything will be just fine. Carol Ann and I will do great together." He nodded and watched her thoughtfully as she walked away.

It's what we have in common that counts.

Use humor in your class by telling about and laughing at things you have done that illustrate a point or help kids to see you as a real person.

Remember that Jesus wants to break in on your students' lives every Sunday morning. Pray that revelation will happen today for each of them.

Watch for opportunities to put students in groups with kids they don't know well. This will help build new relationships in your class and outside of it.

Heidi went to the church office and asked if she could use the phone to call for a ride home. When she was finished, she walked to the entryway to wait. This would be a good time to figure out what to do about Carol Ann.

"Hi, Heidi," said Carol Ann. "I'm waiting for my grandma to pick me up. I'm sorry about the interview. I'm sure I'll get better with practice." Heidi didn't answer immediately. Carol Ann went on hesitantly, "Unless you think I should do something else until I learn more about interviewing and writing?"

Heidi was surprised that she didn't feel as happy as she should. This was her way out, and yet it just didn't feel right. What should she do? What would you do?

What should Heidi do?

Divide the class into small discussion groups. Read today's Memory Verse to the class before beginning the discussion. Hand out copies of the questions. After their discussion, ask each group to role-play how they would have answered Carol Ann.

- ♦ Why was Heidi uncomfortable with the pastoral interview?
- ♦ How could Heidi have helped Carol Ann in the interview?
- ♦ What do you think was Heidi's real problem with Carol Ann?
- ♦ How does the Holy Spirit help us with friendships?
- ♦ In light of today's Memory Verse, how would you advise Heidi?

©1998 CharismaLife Publishers. Permission is granted to reproduce this story — not for resale.

Materials: Copies of Lesson 4 Secret Orders.

Last week you were doing a bit of research on some of the things that you and your friends have in common. Now I want you to do some in-depth research into yourself. That's right, a little bit of spying on old Numero Uno. It is always good to check out your own heart.

Think about some of the things you are good at—sometimes people call them gifts, talents or natural abilities. Write them down. Then next to them, decide how you could use the talents God gave to you to serve His kingdom.

Don't be modest. Tell us what good things God has put in your life. Remember to bring your completed Secret Orders to class next week.

SECRET ORDERS
Think about the things you are good at and write them down. Next to them write how you could use these talents God has given you to serve His kingdom.

ACTIVITIES CHART

Galatians: Treasure Hunt for Freedom

Each activity brings home the Power Point, Memory Verse or one emphasis of the Bible Lesson.

m = Memory Verse Activity *w = Worksheet Activity* *r = Reproducible Page*

Week	Drama	Music	Creative Writing	Bible Study	Individual Art	Group Art	Object Lesson	Cooking	Game	Problem Solving	Outreach Project	Challenge Review	Discussion
1			✔(w)		✔(w)		✔		✔(m)	✔		✔(r)	✔
2		✔(w)		✔(w)		✔		✔	✔(m)			✔(r)	✔
3	✔(w)				✔(m)				✔(w)	✔	✔	✔(r)	✔
4				✔	✔	✔(m)			✔(w)	✔(w)		✔(r)	✔
5	✔(w)			✔(w)			✔		✔(m)	✔		✔(r)	✔
6		✔(w)	✔			✔		✔	✔(m, w)			✔(r)	✔
7			✔(w)	✔(m)			✔		✔		✔(w)	✔(r)	✔
8			✔(w)	✔(m)	✔(w)		✔(w)		✔	✔		✔(r)	✔
9	✔(w, m)		✔		✔(w)			✔	✔			✔(r)	✔
10		✔	✔(w)	✔(w)	✔(m)				✔			✔(r)	✔
11	✔				✔(w)		✔		✔(m)	✔(w)		✔(r)	✔
12			✔(w)	✔(m)		✔		✔(w)	✔		✔	✔(r)	✔
13		✔(w)		✔		✔(w)			✔(m)	✔		✔(r)	✔

ITEMS NEEDED FOR LESSON

❏ Challenge notebooks
❏ Lesson 4 Secret Orders

1—Bible Study
❏ *Club 56 Activity Zone* page 9
❏ Bibles
❏ Pencils

❏ Index cards
❏ Pens

2—Drama Activity
❏ *Club 56 Activity Zone* page 10
❏ Bibles
❏ Concordance
❏ Pencils

❏ Bibles
❏ Index cards
❏ Pens

3—Object Lesson
❏ None

4—Problem Solving
❏ Index cards
❏ Pen

❏ Index cards (six)
❏ Pen

❏ None

❏ Copies of Lesson 5 Secret Orders

SPECIAL NOTE

Have you ever thought about the fact that each week as you are imparting God's Word into the lives of your students, others are doing the same thing around the world? Spend some time this week praying for others who are ministering to 5th and 6th graders in the same way you are. Ask God to do a work in their lives that will encourage their students to take a stand for our Lord. It could change our world!

Faith is taking God at His Word.

I do not live anymore—it is Christ living in me. I still live in my body, but I live by faith in the Son of God. He loved me and gave himself to save me.

Galatians 2:20

John 1:12; Acts 15:9; Romans 5:1; Galatians 2:20; 3:14; Ephesians 2:8; 1 Peter 1:5;

A. Which Came First?
B. You Gotta Have Faith!
C. It's All You'll Ever Need!

YOU GOTTA HAVE FAITH

I was 4 years old when I asked the Lord to forgive me of my sins and make me a part of His family. I had been caught telling lies to my brothers and parents and knew I needed forgiveness and help if I was ever going to be able to break such a nasty habit. I clearly remember my father sitting on the edge of my bed one night as I repeated the sinner's prayer—kid style.

After we said amen, I started crying and told my dad I needed to tell Mom the news. She was already in bed so I ran to where she was and proclaimed, "I'm forgiven. Jesus loves me, and I'm going to be with Him forever."

I know that April evening was the most important night of my life. There was never a time in my young childhood, teenage years or early adulthood when I questioned whether God had heard my prayer. I knew that I was right with Him and was assured of His salvation and forgiveness whenever I needed it. I took Him at His Word at the age of 4 and never needed to pray a recommitment prayer or repeat the process out of doubt.

The students in your class need to know where they stand with the Lord. Salvation is not a request which needs to be restated every year, at every summer camp or each time the teacher offers an opportunity. Teach your 5th and 6th grade students that they can take God at His Word. When they put stock in the promises of eternal life and forgiveness made possible through Jesus, they can know beyond the shadow of a doubt that God will keep up His end of the bargain. They can keep their end of the bargain by living out the faith that drew them to the Lord in the first place.

Materials: Challenge notebooks and Lesson 4 Secret Orders.

Ask a few of your students to share with the class what they think their talents are and how God can use them to help others learn about Him Have the students place their completed Secret Orders in their Challenge notebooks.

Materials: Index cards and pens.

Before class: Print the following occupations on individual index cards: coach, fireman, ringmaster, surgeon, electrician and lawyer. Make a card for each student, creating duplicate sets if needed or use your own ideas.

There are important materials or tools for just about every profession. Do you think you can identify the most important piece of machinery or material for a few common professions? **Let's test your skills.** Give each student a card. Let the students know there is no right or wrong answers for this activity, but the students should be able to defend why the item they chose is the most important. When the students share their answers, allow other members of the class to challenge them if they think they have a better idea.

You came up with some interesting answers. Now, turn your card over and print the word *Christian* on your card.

♦ What do you think would be the most important thing for a Christian to have to live his life effectively? You may chose an item, characteristic or quality to answer this one. The students' answers will vary, but give them time to share and explain their suggestions.

Today we will be talking about faith—something a Christian can't afford to leave home without.

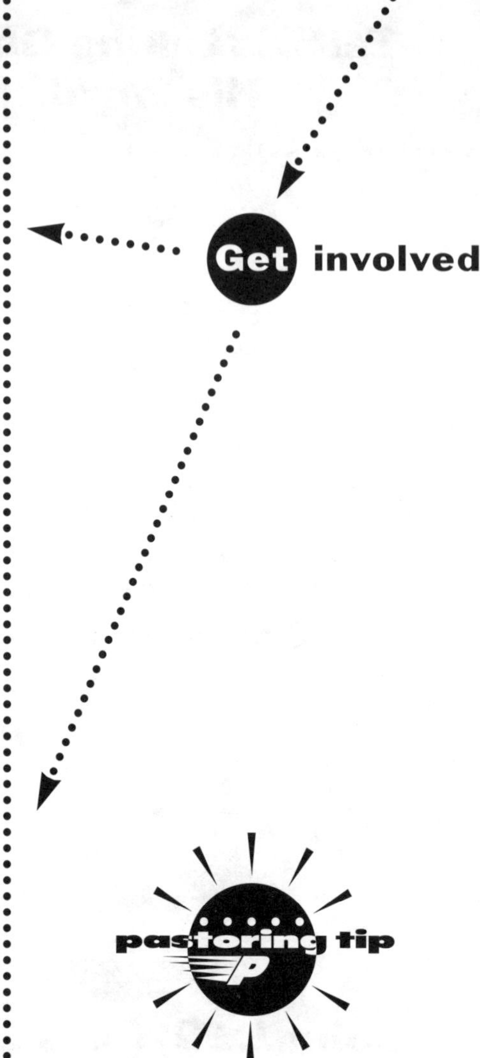

Use the answers the students give in the second part of this activity to help you understand the spiritual maturity of your class. Pay close attention to their responses so you can teach them more effectively.

Faith is taking God at His Word.

Materials: Bibles, index cards and pens.

Before class: Print each of the following Scripture references on individual index cards: Ephesians 2:8; John 1:12; Romans 5:1; Galatians 3:14; Acts 15:9 and 1 Peter 1:5.

Which Came First?

There's an old riddle which asks the question, "Which came first—the chicken or the egg?" What do you think is the correct answer and why? *(Allow several students to answer.)* Many of us would say the chicken came first because we believe God made chickens when He created the earth. Here's another question for you to think about and answer:

♦ **Does faith come before or after salvation?**

I know that sounds like a pretty deep question, and there are a few other things we need to talk about before we can understand the answer, but give it a try. What do you think? *(Allow several students to share. Pay attention to their answers to give you hints about their understanding of faith and salvation).*

In reality, faith comes before salvation and after salvation. It's important that we have a good definition of faith before we go any further in our lesson.

♦ **What is faith?** *Believing or trusting; knowing something will happen.*

During our time today, we will define faith as it is explained in our Power Point: ***Faith is taking God at His Word.*** God tells us how to be saved and how to live a Christ-centered life. Faith means doing what He says and living with the belief that He means every word.

Before we can ever receive salvation from God and be forgiven of our sins, we must believe God is who He says He is and that His Son Jesus died in our place. We have to have faith that we really will be forgiven of our sins when we repent. So in that way, faith comes before salvation. If we don't have faith in the first place, we'll never actually turn to God and turn away from the sin in which we've been living.

You Gotta Have Faith!

That's not the only reason we need to have faith. We also must have faith if we're going to be successful as Christians. When things go wrong in your life, you're mistreated or you want to go along with the crowd and do something that doesn't please God, what is it that is going to keep you on track? Faith. Faith that God's Word is true, that He knows you, is there for you and wants you to do what is right. Faith that God is taking care of you and is going to reward you for your faithfulness. When you blow it and give into temptation and sin or go against what God wants, what is it that will bring you back to Him and ask for forgiveness rather than give up forever? Faith.

Faith that He still loves you and will forgive you no matter what. Faith that you can do better next time and stand up for what is right.

Faith is a crucial part of the Christian life. None of us would get very far with God if we didn't have faith. Many of you wouldn't even be in this class.

♦ **After hearing all of this, what role would you say faith has played in your life?** *(Let several students share their experiences. Encourage them to share about their salvation at this time, too.)*

Living for Christ isn't always easy. There are times when it is downright tough. The Holy Spirit living and working inside of you provides some of the strength you will need. Making up your mind and exerting your will to do what is right is also a big part of being a Christian. When you combine those two factors with faith, you have what it takes to live for Christ.

♦ **Who from the Bible needed faith in order to accomplish what God had for them to do?**

♦ **Who made decisions based on their faith in God?**

♦ **Who from history made decisions based on their faith in God?**

♦ **When have you made a decision based on your faith in God?**

It's All You'll Ever Need!

Faith is one of those gifts from God that keeps on giving. There are many benefits that are ours when we have faith and live out our faith as believers. Scripture in the Old and New Testament tells about the different things we can receive from God through our faith. For now, let's look at a few verses in the New Testament.

(Have the students choose partners. Distribute index cards to each pair. Have the students locate their verse(s) in their Bibles and identify the thing that is received by faith. Inform the students that the words belief *and* trust *are used throughout their verses as other words for faith. The words students will be looking for are as follows: Eph. 2:8—saved; John 1:12—right; Rom. 5:1—made right; Gal. 3:14—Spirit; Acts 15:9—pure hearts; 1 Pet. 1:5 – keeps you safe. Have students share their findings with the rest of the class.)*

♦ **Why do you think each of the things we identified would enable us to live for Christ?**

♦ **How do you think the item you identified would be a benefit to a 5th or 6th grader?**

♦ **When have you, as a 5th or 6th grader, already benefited from the items each pair identified?**

Many of our spiritual needs as Christians can be met when we have faith that God will do what He says. Remember what our Power Point says—*Faith is taking God at His Word.*

Conclusion

Considering how important faith is to our daily relationship with the Lord, it's a wise thing to ask God to help us exercise our faith. We can use our faith when we pray for our friends and relatives who don't yet have a relationship with the Lord. That is just one way we can exercise and express our

Track the number of times you call on the same students. Make an effort to direct questions to all your students rather than just to the ones who are anxious to speak.

Faith is taking God at His Word.

faith. We know that faith helps us receive God and take Him at His Word, so let's pray right now in faith that the people we care about who don't know the Lord would have the same kind of faith we do.

(Have the students think of one person they know who is not saved. Ask them to pray silently for that person. Next ask your students to examine their own lives to see where they have not been taking God at His Word. Have each student identify one area, relationship or circumstance they are facing in which they are having a tough time having faith in God to help. Ask them to agree with you as you pray for their needs.)

Dear Lord, we love You and are so thankful that You have given us the opportunity to know You and be freed of sin through our relationship with Your Son, Jesus. We believe You are who You say You are, and we take You at Your Word. Please help us in the areas where we are weak and have a hard time putting our faith in You. Help us when we struggle, and help us to hear from You and take You at Your Word. We love You. In Jesus' name, amen.

Galatians 2:20

I do not live anymore—it is Christ living in me. I still live in my body, but I live by faith in the Son of God. He loved me and gave himself to save me.

Materials: Index cards (six) and pens.

Before class: Write one section of the Memory Verse on each index card as follows:
- ◊ I do not live anymore—
- ◊ it is Christ living in me.
- ◊ I still live in my body,
- ◊ But I live by faith in the Son of God.
- ◊ He loved me
- ◊ and gave himself to save me.

We are going to learn today's Memory Verse in a different way. I have a section of the verse written on each of these cards. I am going to choose six volunteers who would each like to act out one card. Choose your six students, give them the cards and give them about 2-3 minutes to decide how they will act out the statement. Let's say the verse once while our actors are planning their presentations. Each person is going to present their statement and our job is to place them in the correct order after we see them and decide what their part of the verse says. Allow them to act out their section one at a time while the rest of the class determines what part of the verse they have. Now that we have them in order, let's say the verse a few more times while they act out each section.

1—Bible Study

Materials: *Club 56 Activity Zone* page 9, Bibles and pencils.

Note: This activity needs to be finished before doing the drama activity.

The Bible is loaded with accounts of people who took God at His Word, placed their faith in Him and believed the promises He made. The book of Hebrews has an entire chapter dedicated to these people—a real "Hall of Fame" of sorts. With a closer look we can find out how taking God at His Word can radically change our lives. Take a walk through the Hall of Fame with a friend and see what you can discover about the people honored there. Read the Scripture reference on each statue and fill out the appropriate plaque for each person, listing the person's name, claim to fame and result of his faithfulness.

Distribute the activity pages and allow the students to work in pairs to complete the activity. Have each pair share their findings with the rest of the class, then follow up with the questions below.

♦ Which person do you admire most? Why?

♦ How would your life be different if you had the faith this person had?

♦ How would having more faith affect a tough situation in your life?

♦ What can you do today to let God know you are taking Him at His Word?

2—Drama

Materials: *Club 56 Activity Zone* page 10, Bibles, concordance and pencils.

Note: The Bible Study activity must be completed first.

I hope you all listened closely while we were going over the page for our last activity, because now you will have an opportunity to act on what you learned. Direct the students to the instructions at the top of their pages. Students can work in the same pairs as the previous activity to create their skits. Have each pair choose a character to be the focus of their interview. Allow each pair time to create and rehearse their skits and then present them to the class. Students may use their Bibles and a concordance to gather more information about the person they chose. Have other pairs guess the identity of the Hall of Famer in each skit after it is presented.

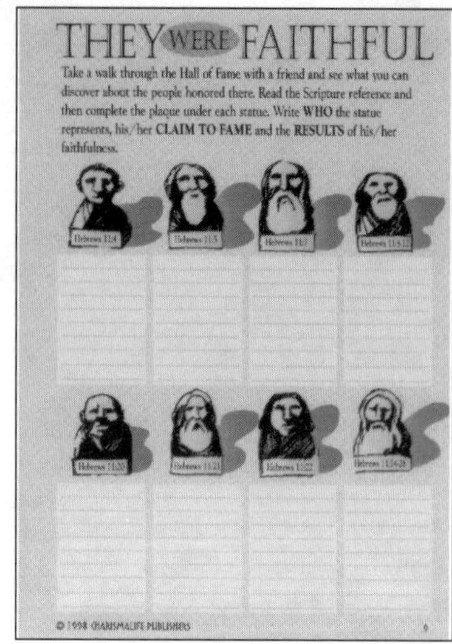

Activity Zone page 9

Make notes in your *Club 56 Leader's Manual* about which activities worked best with your class. This will help you plan lessons more effectively in the future.

Activity Zone page 10

Faith is taking God at His Word.

3—Object Lesson

Materials: None.

Ask the students to find partners. Then instruct one student in each pair to put his hands down at his side. Have his partner face him and press on the backs of the his hands. As the partner presses in, the student is to push up as hard as possible. Time this for 30 seconds. Then have the partners let go. The student's arms should automatically rise up on their own. Switch roles so both partners can experience this.

♦ **What happened to your arms?** *They floated up by themselves.*

♦ **What caused this to happen?** Students may guess at the cause but most will not know.

In our experiment, we found that something caused our arms to rise. We know there was a reason it happened, even though we couldn't see it with our eyes. It was real even though we couldn't touch it.

♦ **What other things do you feel or experience and know are real even without seeing or touching them?** *Love, honesty, gravity, surface tension, etc.*

Faith is the same! We may not actually be able to see God, but we can still experience Him. We know from the things that happen around us and in us that He is real!

4—Problem Solving

Materials: Index cards and pen.

Before class: Write each situation listed below on an index card.

1. A friend's mother and baby sister are seriously hurt in a car accident. When you ask your friend if you can pray together, he says he doesn't know much about God. He has never talked to Him and is not sure He even exists.

2. You ask a girl in school to come to church with you. She says she can't because her dad doesn't believe in all that religious junk. He says it is only for weak people who can't make it on their own. Her family is wealthy, healthy and happy. They can take care of themselves.

You gotta have faith! How many times are we told that? When we have doubts or questions, we may hear someone tell us these words. In our lesson, we talked about faith.

♦ **What is faith?**

♦ **What can you do if you do not have faith or your faith is weak?** *Pray to God to give you faith or to increase your faith.*

Sometimes, we are faced with some tough situations. How we handle them depends on our faith.

Divide the class into two groups. Give each group one of the situation cards. Ask the groups to read the situation and then discuss possible ways they would

Give students time to talk about their interests and hobbies with one another at some point during class time. The relationships they build with one another will help them enjoy class time more.

respond. After several minutes of discussion, ask the groups to share their situations and responses. Then discuss the following:

♦ Do you think it is easier to have faith during good times or bad times? Why?

♦ What obstacles can hinder faith when everything in life is going well? when things are going wrong?

♦ What can we do when our faith is wavering?

"Look, Devante," said his mother, "sometimes you just have to have faith. I can't explain why I believe in God, it just happened in my heart one day. Why are you asking?" He just shook his head and looked down. Devante didn't know if he could explain his dilemma to his mother. By his estimation she had been a Christian forever. How could she understand what he was going through?

"Mom," he questioned, "would you be sad if I decided that I'm not really a Christian?"

His mother sat down at the dining room table and patted the chair next to her. "Sit down, Devante. First, yes, I would be sad. But I don't want you to make a decision about being a Christian because of how I feel. I want you to know that you know Jesus is your Savior. You know what, Devante? I have so much faith in God that I believe He will prove to you that He is God. May I pray with you?"

He hesitated for only a minute and then said, "Sure. But Mom, I want you to pray that I believe in God just like I believe that you are real, OK?" She laughed, "I will, Devante, and I believe that God will make Himself very real to you."

The next day Devante's Sunday School teacher asked the class to share some of their experiences with God. "You know, class, hearing what other people have faced and how God helped them in their difficulties helps strengthen our faith." Devante looked around the room at the class of kids. He doubted that any of them had a whole lot to say. Devante had a feeling that they were like him; everything he knew about God came from his mother. In fact, it seemed like God was really more for older people than kids. What could a kid tell about God that might help him?

Stop here.

Ask the students to take a minute and think about their personal experiences with God. Invite them to share anything that might encourage another 5th or 6th grader in his faith.

The rest of the story: Devante sat stunned as he heard story after story about how God did wonderful things for the kids in the class. Suddenly, he began to remember times that he had prayed and God had answered in powerful ways. How had he forgotten? The teacher looked around the room and asked if anyone else had something to share.

Thank students for sharing their thoughts. Do this privately as they leave class if they are shy so you do not embarrass them.

What should Devante do?

♦ Should Devante share with the class what God did for him?

♦ How does sharing with others our personal experiences encourage them?

Faith is taking God at His Word.

 Materials: Copies of Lesson 5 Secret Orders.

We all need to have people that we look up to—even in the spy business. I mean, personally, I think Sherlock Holmes is the greatest—so cool and classy. He gave those of us in the detective business a good name.

Hebrews 11 talks about some of the great heroes of the Bible. Your assignment this week is to read through that chapter and then come up with the qualities you think are needed to be a hero. Also name a several people who are heroes to you. These could be people you know or maybe people you could only hope to meet.

Remember to bring your completed Secret Orders to class next week.

SECRET ORDERS
Read Hebrews 11 this week and come up with some qualities of a hero. Name several people who are heroes to you.

SUGGESTED SCHEDULE

The following is a suggested time schedule for using *Club 56* in a one hour and 15 minute class time. If you have more time, have the class do additional activities. There is more than enough material from which to choose in building your lesson plans.

MINUTES:

5	Challenge Review
5	Opening Activity
15	Bible Lesson
5	Memory Verse Activity

MINUTES:

25	More Activities
15	Living It Out
5	Challenge for the Week

BIBLE TO USE

We recommend that you use the International Children's Bible (ICB) translation of Scripture. It is easy to understand, is a direct translation and uses words that are familiar to 5th and 6th graders.

In both the *Leader's Manual* and *Activity Zone*, all quotations, Memory Verses and Scripture references are taken from the ICB.

CHALLENGE INCENTIVES

Most 5th and 6th graders need a reminder to complete the outside assignment of a Challenge. Here are some ideas to help them remember to do the assignment and bring their Secret Orders back each week.

♦ Read and complete Secret Orders yourself. Take the Challenge each week and bring yours back.

♦ Offer small, edible treats each week during the Challenge Review for those who bring back their Secret Orders.

♦ Develop a point system for the entire class. Each student who brings back his Secret Orders receives points. This will reward the entire class. Ask the students to decide with you what reward would be appropriate.

♦ Students can exchange phone numbers to call and remind each other throughout the week.

♦ Call various students during the week to see how they are doing on their Challenges.

Club 56

SUGGESTED SCOPE & SEQUENCE

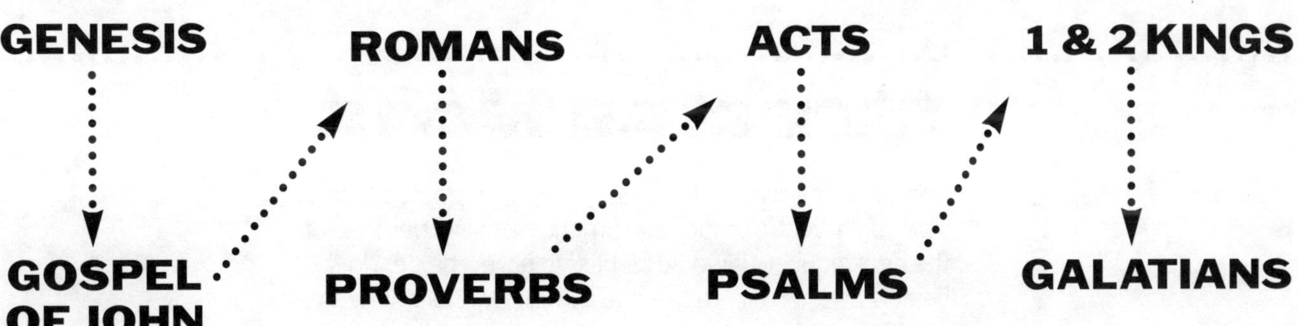

ITEMS NEEDED FOR LESSON

☐ Challenge notebooks
☐ Lesson 5 Secret Orders

1—Creative Writing

☐ Paper
☐ Pencils (colored)
☐ Tape

☐ Games (board games, card games, etc.)
☐ Game pieces (several)
☐ Watch with second hand
☐ Paper
☐ Pens

2—Music

☐ *Club 56 Activity Zone* page 11
☐ Watch with second hand
☐ Pencils

3—Group Art

☐ Paper   ☐ Pencils
☐ Newsprint   ☐ Markers
☐ Tape

☐ Bibles
☐ "The World as Best as I Remember It, Part 2" by Rich Mullins
☐ CD (or cassette) player
☐ Invitations (homemade or purchased)
☐ Paper
☐ Pens

4—Cooking

☐ Lollipop sticks (18)   ☐ Candy thermometer
☐ Margarine (1/4 cup)   ☐ Hot plate
☐ Corn syrup (1/2 cup light) ☐ Candy hearts
☐ Sugar (3/4 cup)   ☐ Flavoring (if desired)
☐ Food coloring   ☐ Measuring spoons
☐ Cooking spray (nonstick) ☐ Measuring cups
☐ Cookie sheet   ☐ Paper
☐ Sauce pan (small)   ☐ Pens
☐ Wooden spoon   ☐ Chalkboard
                            ☐ Chalk

☐ *Club 56 Activity Zone* page 12
☐ Pencils

☐ None

☐ Copies of Lesson 6 Secret Orders

SPECIAL NOTE

The fourth activity in today's lesson is a cooking activity. Make sure you have the proper equipment. Likewise, because of the heat required, it would be best to have a helper do the heating part. You can go over the Living It Out story while the liquid is being heated.

Calling all people: God's family is for you.

But when the right time came, God sent his Son. His Son was born of a woman and lived under the law. God did this so that he could buy freedom for those who were under the law. His purpose was to make us his children.

Galatians 4:4-5

Genesis 15:5-6; Galatians 3:6-9

A. You Mean Abraham Saw Me?

B. RSVP Accordingly

C. Hangin' Out or Being a Part?

GOD WANTS YOU AND YOU AND EVERYONE

From the earliest time I can remember, I have always felt wanted by my parents. Being the youngest of four children, I remember times when money was scarce, there were more mouths to feed than there was food and one-on-one attention was a rare experience. In spite of all this, I grew up secure and confident in the place I held in my parents' hearts. I grew up believing that I had helped complete the family. I was given to my parents and brothers because they needed me and I needed them. I was never treated as one of many, but instead was taught I was significant to the life of our family.

I know that for many people, this may not be the case. We often spend our lives searching for a way to be a part of the group, make a difference and hold a position of importance. Belonging to God's family fills our need for all three. God has called each of us and has carved a place for our gifts, talents and unique personalities to not only be accepted, but also to flourish. God's kingdom is indeed for all of us. We are a part of His family and key players in assuring that His plans will be accomplished.

Remind your students that they are a part of God's family for the long haul. He has extended an invitation to each of them to be called His child. He knows them by name, understands their needs and concerns and is filled with love towards them. If there are children in your class who have not yet become a part of God's family, use the lesson to help them understand the invitation. Teach them how to RSVP and become a member of His household. There is always room for one more.

Materials: Challenge notebooks and Lesson 5 Secret Orders.

Last week our challenge was to read Hebrews 11 and decide on the qualities of a hero. Let's share a few of those characteristics before we begin our new lesson. Have the students place their completed Secret Orders in their Challenge notebooks.

Materials: Games (board games, card games, etc.), game pieces (several), watch with second hand, paper and pens.

Note: Game pieces can be found in most board games.

♦ **If we were to hold a game-playing marathon this morning, what games would be conducive to play with the number of students in our class?** Answers will vary based on your class. Smaller classes may list games like cards, charades, etc. Larger classes may list games like soccer, football, kickball, etc. Display the games you have brought to class to help trigger ideas.

Divide students into pairs and distribute a piece of paper and a pen to each pair. **I am going to ask you and your partner to make a list of games which meet certain requirements. Your team will have about two minutes to add as many games to each list as possible. The first list you will be creating will be for games needing up to four players. You may include specific sports in your answers. Begin.** Give students two minutes to write. **The next category is games which need 20 to 50 players. Again, you may list specific sports among your answers.** Give students two minutes to write. **Your final list is to consist of all the games you can think of which require 50 or more players. And guess what? You can use specific sports as part of your answers.** Give students two minutes to write.

Have each pair read their list aloud. If students can justify any debatable answer, give them credit. Award a game piece as a reward to the pair with the most games listed, one for each of the three lists. **What if I were to tell the class that for the rest of our time today we will be playing a game in which only the people with playing pieces are allowed to participate?**

♦ How would the people without pieces feel?

♦ How would the pairs with pieces decide who gets to play?

♦ How would the people with pieces feel?

Calling all people: God's family is for you.

This lesson can be powerful for those who come from families where they are the only Christians. Show special sensitivity to these members of your class today.

The good news is, we are not playing any such game. We are, however, going to discuss a team you can participate in which has no limit to the number of players allowed. In fact, it's less like a team and more like a family. Our Power Point today is—*Calling all people: God's family is for you.*

Materials: Bibles, "The World As Best As I Remember It, Part 2" by Rich Mullins, CD (or cassette) player, invitations (homemade or purchased), paper and pens.

Note: If you do not own the recording listed above, check with several people in your church to borrow one or contact your local Christian bookstore.

Before class: Familiarize yourself with the song listed above so you can easily point out the verse students need to pay close attention to (verse two). Have the recording prepared to play "Sometimes by Step" before the students arrive. Fill out an invitation for each student with the following information (purchased invitations will be worded differently, so fill yours out accordingly):

You are invited to: Become a part of God's family
Time: For the rest of your life (and after)
Place: Here on earth and later in heaven
Given By: God through His Son, Jesus
RSVP: As soon as possible

You Mean Abraham Saw Me?

We've already started talking about being a part of God's family. In previous lessons we have discussed how important it is to put our faith in what God says and take Him at His Word. What I'm about to share with you may seem unreal for a few moments, but think about it, and I think it will start to mean a lot to you.

I'm going to play a song for you that talks about you and me and our lives as Christians. The person singing is reflecting on his faith and the way his relationship with the Lord has strengthened his life. He goes on to state his commitment to follow God forever.

The part I want you to pay close attention to is when he mentions a man from the Old Testament. This part will come in the second verse. See if you can catch what he is saying. *(Play the song for the class. If you are not using the recording, read Gen. 15:5-6. You will be able to lead the discussion using the following questions based on these verses.)*

- ♦ Who is the person mentioned in the song?

- ♦ What comment does the artist make about Abraham? *When Abraham looked into the heavens and saw the stars, God was showing him that one of the stars symbolized his life. (If you are not using the recording, you will want to make this point at this time.)*

That is pretty amazing to think about, isn't it? The fact is, we are all descendants of Abraham. The Bible tells us we are connected to him through the promise God gave him about his descendants. God fulfilled His promise to Abraham in one way by giving him a son—Isaac. He also fulfilled it in another way: He sent Jesus to earth to stand in the gap for all of us and forgive our sins. You'll see what I mean if you read Galatians 3:6-9. *(Have the students turn to this passage in their Bibles. Ask a volunteer to read the verses aloud.)*

- ♦ This passage says that the true children of Abraham are those who what? *Have faith.*

- ♦ What is the benefit for all those who believe as Abraham believed? *They will be blessed.*

It can almost be mind-boggling to think that we are spiritually children of Abraham because of our faith. Think about it. When God directed Abraham to look up to the stars, he saw one twinkling that stood for you, David and Mary. He saw one for Felecia and Brandon, too. You are a part of the Bible. You're mentioned!

The blessing we share with Abraham is that we can be saved. We are made a part of God's family when we turn to Him and have faith in what His Son, Jesus, accomplished on the cross.

RSVP Accordingly

So, what do we do with the fact that we have an opportunity to become a part of the family of God? Remember as we read earlier, this is not an invitation that was originally extended to us. We aren't Jews—and they are who were originally supposed to be accepted into the family of God. Now we are a part of God's grand scheme of things, and He wants us to respond to Him. Some of you have already responded to this opportunity, and some of you may not have understood the invitation. Some of you may have asked Jesus to forgive you of your sins, but don't really feel like a family member. What should you do now? Let's see if we can come up with some ideas as to how we should respond to God's invitation to be part of His family.

(Hand out the invitations. Allow the students to choose a way a typical 5th or 6th grader might RSVP to the opportunity to become a part of God's family. Have each student tell you which type of RSVP she intends to send: Responding for the first time or responding in order to obtain family connections that may have been overlooked before. Encourage students to make the responses balanced, with some students choosing each of the options, not everyone choosing the same one. Hand out paper and pens and give students time to write letters to God in response to the invitation. Have them include how they feel about the opportunity and how they think it will affect their lives on earth and in heaven. Have the students read their responses to the rest of the class if they are comfortable doing so.)

God wants us to come to Him sincerely. He wants us to be honest with Him about our questions. If we don't know what it means to be a part of His

Stay sharp! The comments and questions from students, which sometimes lead to rabbit trails, can be incorporated into the lesson if you know where you are going. Redirect conversation to the Power Point whenever possible. Yes, Brian, it is hard when your family isn't Christian—that's why our Power Point is so important.

Don't grow weary in work you are doing as a Sunday School teacher. If you feel like your lessons are going nowhere, talk with your assistant and strategize about what can be changed, enhanced or eliminated to make your time in the classroom more successful.

Calling all people: God's family is for you.

family, He wants us to ask Him. He has given us parents, teachers, friends and pastors to help us, too.

He also wants everyone to come. Unlike families here on earth, God doesn't run out of space or money. He desires that everyone would make the decision to become one of His children. He never gets too busy for any of His children or too occupied with who already knows Him not to notice the prayer of another person wanting to make herself right with Him. As our Power Point says—*Calling all people: God's family is for you.*

Hangin' Out or Being a Part?

When you ask to be a part of God's family, it happens! All it takes is that faith we were talking about earlier. You have to have faith in what God says, especially the fact that He sent His Son, Jesus, to die for our sins so we wouldn't have to pay for them ourselves. You are a full-fledged member of God's family when you do this. You can't earn your way into His family or advance to a higher status in the family by doing good things or trying really hard. It's like in your own family, you will always be the son or daughter of your parents. You can't apply for an advancement or different position in the family.

There is nothing better than to be a son or daughter in God's family. That's the same relationship Jesus has with God! You are brothers and sisters of Christ and in Christ. You are joint heirs with Jesus! Wow!

Where are you today? Are you used to thinking of yourself as a person who has been forgiven by God, but not much more important than that? Are you unsure of your status at all because you've never asked Jesus to be your Lord and Savior? Today is the day for a radical change. You don't have to just hang out with the family of God: you can be an actual part of what's going on. *(Encourage students to take a few minutes to get by themselves somewhere in the room. On the back of the RSVP they wrote earlier, have them write a personal RSVP to God. Ask them to write with total honesty, as these letters will not be read by anyone.)*

Conclusion

Knowing that we are a part of God's family can do a lot for our feelings of self-worth. There is nothing greater we could ever be. When we feel insignificant or discouraged, we can remind ourselves of our faith in God and realize again that we are His children and He is looking out for us. He knows you, your needs and the plans He has for your life. Talk to Him today. Share with Him the letters you just wrote. Read them aloud sometime today in the privacy of your room or while you take a walk outside. I'm going to pray for each of you now before you go. Please pray along with me.

Dear Lord, we are thankful we can call You Father. You have made a way for us to be your sons and daughters, and we are so thankful. Thank You for not running out of room in Your heart or Your plans for each of us. You are a good and loving Father, and we want to know better how to be Your children. Thank You for giving us a place to belong and a family to call our own. We love You. In Jesus' name, amen.

Materials: *Club 56 Activity Zone* page 12 and pencils.

Two people are chosen as captains for the kickball team. They begin to take turns choosing players. You nervously wait to see when you will be picked, afraid you'll be the last person anybody wants for their team.

With God, you don't have to worry about being unwanted. As the title of today's lesson tells us, God wants you and you and everyone! God desires for everyone to be part of His family. We all have different talents and gifts to serve others.

We are going to play a game which shows different ways we serve others. Hand out the activity pages and pencils. Read the directions together. Emphasize that they must ask each person if they have performed a specific service. The students are not to just volunteer the answers without being asked. They must move on to another person after asking one question. They can then return to that individual later.

After the students have played the game for five minutes, discuss the outcomes with the group:

♦ Were you able to fill up all of the boxes?

♦ Which boxes were easiest to fill? Which were most difficult?

♦ What are some other ways in which we can serve others?

1—Creative Writing

Materials: Paper, pencils (colored) and tape.

How many of you have ever seen a flyer on a wall advertising a special event? Have the students share their experiences. What was it about the flyer that caught your eye? Was it the colors? the words used to describe the event? the way or place where it was hung? Your assignment for the next few minutes is to design a flyer advertising the hugest reunion or open house in history for all the members of God's family. You will need to include a description of who is invited, what will happen at the reunion and why everyone should come. Make it bright and colorful.

Give the students time to work on their flyers and then ask them to share what they have created with the class. Hang the flyers in a highly visible area of the church or your classroom.

Galatians 4:4–5

But when the right time came, God sent his Son. His Son was born of a woman and lived under the law. God did this so that he could buy freedom for those who were under the law. His purpose was to make us his children.

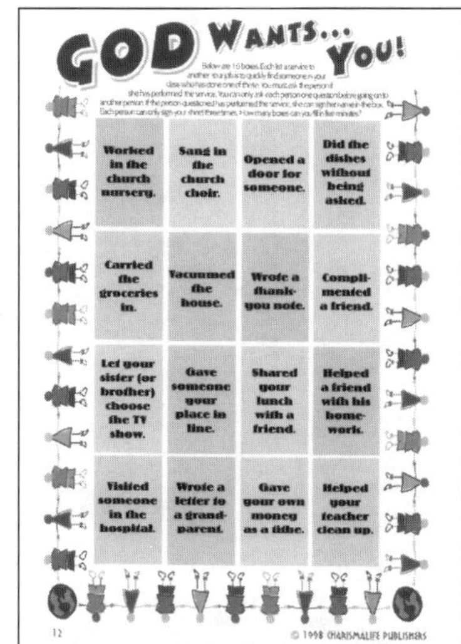

Activity Zone page 12

Displaying the work created by your students communicates that their thoughts and expressions are valuable and appreciated. They will enjoy seeing what they have created and sharing it with their friends and family when they visit the class.

Activity Zone page 11

Never assume that all your students have had a salvation experience. Listen to the conversations and observe students as they work on their illustrations for clues as to the understanding and acceptance of salvation.

2—Music

Materials: *Club 56 Activity Zone* page 11, watch with second hand and pencils.

We've learned today there is room for everyone in God's family. Thinking about that reminds me of one of my favorite songs, "He's Got the Whole World in His Hands." Ask the class members to sing the chorus of the song if they remember it. If not, sing it for them.

One of the fun things to do with this song is to make up other verses with different people or groups. Your challenge for the next five minutes is to see how many different people or groups your team can come up with for new verses. Just about any answer will be acceptable because, as we learned in today's lesson, God's family is for everyone.

Have the students get into two teams. Give each team five minutes to list their answers. Have the teams count their answers to see who has the most listed. Have the teams cross off people or groups shared by both teams and determine the winning team based on the longer list remaining. Have each team sing the song with their four most unusual or creative entries.

3—Group Art

Materials: Paper, newsprint, tape, pencils and markers.

Before class: Label a large section of newsprint, "Adoption Day Memories." Hang the newsprint on a wall in your classroom.

When you think about it, everyone in our class is adopted. Some of us may have been adopted by our parents when we were babies, but all of us, if we have asked Jesus to be our Savior, have been adopted into His family. Do you remember the events surrounding the time when you asked Jesus to forgive you of your sins? Do you think you could draw a picture of that time? I think you can!

Distribute the paper, pencils and markers and have the students illustrate the location, day or situation that led to their salvation. Have them place their pictures on the newsprint with tape. When all the pictures have been attached, ask the students to share about what they drew. Provide an opportunity for students who are uncertain of their salvation to pray with you today.

4—Cooking

Materials: Lollipop sticks (18), margarine (1/4 cup), corn syrup (1/2 cup, light), sugar, (3/4 cup), food coloring, cooking spray (nonstick), cookie sheet, sauce pan (small), wooden spoon, candy thermometer, hot plate, candy hearts, flavoring (if desired), measuring spoons, measuring cups, paper, pencils, chalkboard and chalk.

Before class: Have a student with good handwriting write the recipe on the board for others to copy.

Note: Lollipop sticks can be found at any craft store.

When you are older, some of you may choose to serve in the military.

♦ **What are some of the branches of the military?** *Army, Navy, Air Force, Marines, Coast Guard.*

♦ **Do you know anyone in the military? Who? In which branch does she serve?**

When you join any of the military branches, you have to start out in basic training and work your way up. It takes lots of dedication to become a sergeant, captain or commander. If you want any of these top positions, you have to earn them.

♦ **What are some other positions you have to work hard to earn?** *President of a company; captain of a team; principal of a school.*

In our society, we are taught that we have to do great things in order to climb the ladder of success.

♦ **How does this compare with being a Christian?** *Salvation by grace, not our own efforts.*

As we heard in our lesson, we are full-fledged members of God's family the moment we accept Jesus as our Savior. We can't earn our way to acceptance. Now we are going to make some lollipops to help us remember that our acceptance into God's family is an immediate change. As you will see, the sugar and syrup mixture is just a liquid. But when heat is added, it quickly changes form and becomes a new creation. The same thing happens in our lives. When we accept Jesus, we become new creations!

While I prepare the recipe, write it down for your parents to use at home. Complete the following steps to make the lollipops:

1. Spray a cookie sheet with nonstick cooking spray and arrange 18 lollipop sticks on the cookie sheet so that none are touching.

2. Combine 1/4 cup margarine, 1/2 cup light corn syrup and 3/4 cups sugar in a saucepan. Heat to a boil over medium-high heat, stirring frequently.

3. Insert a candy thermometer into the mixture. Continue cooking until the mixture reaches 270 degrees or until a drop of the mixture put into very cold water separates into threads and becomes hard (approximately 8 minutes). Stir to prevent burning and remove from heat.

While the mixture is being stirred, let's go over our Living It Out story.

4. Stir in a drop of food coloring and 1/4 teaspoon of flavoring (if desired).

5. Drop by tablespoon over the end of the sticks. Press on the candy hearts while the lollipops are hardening. Let harden approximately 5 minutes.

Complete the Living It Out story. After the lollipops have hardened, hand them out to your students to enjoy.

Calling all people: God's family is for you.

Arianna glared at her mother. "Don't expect me to give her all my things! This wasn't my idea." Her mother looked at the tape that Arianna had put down to divide her room in half.

"Arianna, this is not the way to welcome someone into our family. Your cousin lost her parents a few years ago, and now Grandma Bolin is very ill. Maria needs a permanent home with a family who will love her. You agreed to this adoption when we talked it over. What's changed?"

"Mom, we barely know her. How do we know that she isn't some kind of serial killer?"

Her mother laughed. "Arianna, Maria will be your sister in every sense of the word. More than anything she longs for a family. When Dad and I flew out there she was so anxious to please us that it made me sad. Dad and I tried to assure her that she didn't need to do anything to win our love."

Arianna sighed, "I just don't see why we need to adopt her. It's so permanent." Another thought came to Arianna. "Hey, what if she does bad things, like steal or lie? We couldn't get rid of her if she's adopted. We'd be stuck with her!" She watched her mother to see if she was finally catching on to the seriousness of their situation.

"Arianna, did you know that you're adopted, too?" Arianna was stunned. What about all those mushy stories they told her about her birth? "Not by Mom and Dad, Arianna, but by God. As Christians we are all adopted into God's family. Do you remember when you felt terrible about lying to Pastor Simms?" Arianna nodded quietly. "What did he tell you after you asked him and Jesus to forgive you?"

Arianna thought about the conversation. "He told me that God forgave me because He loves me." She paused briefly, "He said that no matter what I do, I'm part of God's family and that He will always love me. He said that we might be disciplined for what we do, but that's because God loves us."

Arianna looked at the tape on the floor. *How would I feel if Jesus treated me like I want to welcome Maria?* she wondered. Jesus hadn't kicked her out of His family. But she also wanted Maria to know that she wasn't just going to come here and take over.

How can you help Arianna?

Divide the class into five discussion groups. Assign each group one of the questions listed below. After the discussion ask each group to share their answers with the class.

♦ What seemed to scare Arianna the most about Maria being adopted into their family?

♦ How would you define family?

♦ Is there a difference between your family and God's family? Explain.

- ♦ What advice would you give Arianna about accepting Maria as a sister?

- ♦ Once you're part of the family of God, do you need to do something to remain in the family?

 Materials: Copies of Lesson 6 Secret Orders.

The chief has decided that you are qualified enough for a really tough assignment. You are to be a mole. No, not that furry little creature that likes to dig tunnels but a spy that has been planted deep into dangerous territory.

Your assignment is to watch the members of your family. Find out as much as you can about each of them and their faith. Find out what they believe and where they are with God. Ask them to share with you what they think about the following things: God, heaven, Jesus and the Bible.

Good luck. We will be waiting for your report next week. Remember to bring your completed Secret Orders to class next week.

Calling all people: God's family is for you.

Lesson 6 Secret Orders

ITEMS NEEDED FOR LESSON

❑ Challenge notebooks
❑ Lesson 6 Secret Orders

❑ Newspapers
❑ Index cards
❑ Pens

❑ Bibles
❑ Chalkboard
❑ Chalk

❑ Construction paper
❑ Wrapping (or tissue) paper
❑ Ribbon
❑ Glue
❑ Glitter
❑ Scissors
❑ Pens
❑ Bibles

❑ Copies of Living It Out story

1—Game

❑ Paper
❑ Bibles
❑ Concordance
❑ Pencils

2—Creative Writing

❑ *Club 56 Activity Zone* page 13
❑ Bibles
❑ Pencils

3—Outreach Project

❑ *Club 56 Activity Zone* page 14
❑ Pencils
❑ Envelopes

4—Object Lesson

❑ Twine (heavy, 7 strands, 6 feet each)
❑ Index cards (14)
❑ Tape
❑ Pen
❑ Cans of food (14, large)

❑ Copies of Lesson 7 Secret Orders

SPECIAL NOTE

Club 56 Activity Zone page 13 deals with writing an excerpt from a journal. Journaling is a great way to record what God is doing in your life. You can encourage your students to keep a journal to record different things that happen in their lives.

The law: A foundation for freedom.

This gift is from God, and it is very important to me. If the law could make us right with God, then Christ did not have to die.

Galatians 2:21

Exodus 20–23;
2 Corinthians 5:17;
Galatians 3:13, 24-25;
4:1-4; Ephesians 2:10;
4:24

A. The Law Leads Straight to Christ

B. Splish! Splash! I'm Taking a Bath— Whenever and Wherever!

C. I Sure Clean Up Nicely

LESSON 7

SO, WHY ALL THE RULES IN THE OLD TESTAMENT?

I watched from the rearview mirror as the police officer got into his patrol car. My heart was still racing as the tears I had tried so hard to control began to fall. I was left with a speeding ticket, a fine and a feeling of guilt accompanied with embarrassment. I had blown it, and now I had to call my husband and tell him I had gotten a ticket for speeding. I dialed the cell phone, held my breath and braced for the worst. I expected him to be angry and upset that our insurance rates would increase. I knew our budget was not in a place where 80 dollars would go unnoticed.

I was surprised when Mike answered my distress call with compassionate words. He was concerned with how I was doing and wanted to make sure I wasn't too upset to make the rest of the drive home. Insurance wasn't discussed, no I-told-you-so's were spoken, and I hung up the phone with a sense of relief and gratitude. I knew I had broken the law with my speed and deserved to pay the fine, but Mike's lack of disappointment over my actions softened the sting of my punishment. I felt free of guilt and knew everything would be all right.

God's laws were designed to show us our need for Him. In the Old Testament, men needed to make sacrifices to receive redemption from the Lord. In the New Testament, Jesus paid the ultimate sacrifice for our sins and bought our redemption. In each case, it is God's mercy which makes us right with Him. We all do wrong. We all need forgiveness. We all can come to Him and receive exactly what we need. As believers we are free to seek God for cleansing. He is not concerned with "I-told-you-so's" either. He wants us to be whole and restored, able to do right the next time with the help of the Holy Spirit.

Teach your class about the importance of God's laws and doing what they can to follow them. Then teach them that those laws are in place to show us the incredible gift of freedom they have because they can come to God for forgiveness when they blow it. Jesus has paid the price for each of their lives.

Materials: Challenge notebooks and Lesson 6 Secret Orders.

Discuss what kind of faith your students noticed in their family members. Listen and help them to understand that people are at different places in their spiritual journeys. Encourage them to help their families know more about God's love.

Have the students place their completed Secret Orders in their Challenge notebooks.

Materials: Newspapers, index cards and pens.

Every day newspaper headlines and stories tell of lawbreakers and wrongdoers. If we were to listen to any news report—local, national or worldwide—we would hear about someone's disregard for the law and how his actions affected those around him. Let's take a look at a few papers from this week to find some specifics. Have the students find partners. Give each pair a section of the newspaper and allow two minutes to find an article in that section which tells about someone breaking the law. Have each pair report on their findings. Keep control of the class if an inappropriate article is shared.

♦ What are some of the things that happened to the bystanders in these articles?

♦ Do you think the specific laws in each of the stories were reasonable?

♦ What is one unreasonable law you have heard of in the past?

I don't know about you, but there are a few laws I think I would like to write myself. You know, ones that don't let people take the parking space I've been waiting for, or stores being required to open new checkout lines when the ones that are open are 10 people long. What are some laws you would want to create if you were allowed? Don't answer now; I'm going to give you a chance to write one down in a minute.

Distribute the index cards, one to each student. Give everyone a minute or two to write one law (silly or serious) they would like to see enforced. Tell the students not to write their names on their cards. Collect the cards and read them to the members of the class to see if they would agree with the law or disagree.

Today we're going to do some more talking about laws—not laws made up by 5th and 6th graders, but laws created by God.

Get involved

The law: A foundation for freedom.

Materials: Bibles, chalkboard and chalk.

The Law Leads Straight to Christ

Before the days of Christ, people didn't have the same kind of relationship with God that is available to us today. They could know God and walk closely with Him like many characters of the Old Testament.

♦ **What areas of life do you know of from the Old Testament that were different from the New Testament?** *Animal sacrifices, no relationship with Jesus, etc.*

♦ **What are some of the laws the people of the Old Testament were told to observe?** *(If students have a difficult time identifying these, direct them to the Ten Commandments and other laws found in Ex. 20–23.)*

♦ **What were some of the results when people did not keep these laws as written about in the Old Testament?** *Sometimes they were punished by their leaders. Sometimes they were put to death by God.*

We are really blessed that Jesus changed all of that for us. When God sent His Son, Jesus, to the earth to pay the price for all our sins, He radically changed the life you and I live today, even though Jesus' sacrifice was made 2000 years ago. If we were to take a look at some of the laws the Jews of the Old Testament had to observe, we would begin to feel overwhelmed by the impossibility of doing everything just right. Instead, now that we know Jesus and what He did for us, we can feel overwhelmed with gratitude because we know that without Him we would never be able to make it.

The Holy Spirit makes us aware of our need for Christ even before we ask Him to forgive us of our sins! Think back to the time you asked Jesus to be your Lord and Savior.

♦ **What made you realize you needed to be saved?** *I knew I would go to hell if I didn't ask Jesus into my life; I knew I was a sinner; I knew I needed to be forgiven.*

If you said it was because you didn't want to go to hell, tell me what your life was like before Jesus and why you think you deserved eternal punishment.

People who don't know Jesus aren't forgiven of their sins. They've blown it just like the rest of us, but either they haven't realized it yet, or they haven't decided to give their lives to Jesus. It's when the Holy Spirit shows you that you need Jesus that you even start thinking about giving Him your life. Sin is a very real thing, and it happens every time we don't obey God's laws—any of God's laws. The wild thing is, now that we are in God's family, we have a totally different relationship with Him. All we have to do is ask Him for forgiveness, and He gives it. That's a lot different from the way it was for the people of the Old Testament.

Splish! Splash! I'm Taking a Bath— Whenever and Wherever!

In the Old Testament and all the days before Jesus, men had to make sacrifices and get clearance from a high priest before they were considered cleansed from sin. The law had people pretty much tied up in knots over sin because no one was able to keep it perfectly. The priests were kept quite busy during the specified times of the year when cleansing and forgiveness could take place.

Because of Jesus, the early believers were suddenly able to receive forgiveness at any time, simply by praying and asking God to free them from their sin. Imagine growing up one way for your entire life—buying an animal for a sacrifice, preparing the animal, bringing it to a priest for the sacrifice, going through a bunch of rituals and then getting the OK from the priest that you were forgiven and he'd see you again next time when you would go through the whole process again. Then all of a sudden, everything changes. Now you mess up, talk to God directly and immediately you're restored and back on the right track.

This was a tough thing for the early Christians (most of whom were converted Jews), to grasp. They felt torn between old laws and rituals and the new easier, freer way of doing things. This is why Paul wrote the letter to the Galatians in the first place. Some of the things he said may have seemed pretty harsh, but he didn't want the new Christians, Jews or Gentiles, to be compelled to live by the laws of the Old Testament as some leaders were suggesting.

(Have the students get into three groups. Assign each group one of the following passages: Gal. 3:13; 3:24-25 and 4:1-4. Each group will have two minutes to read their assigned passages and report back to the class the message Paul was giving. They will need to put the verses in their own words. Record what the students say by writing it on the chalkboard.)

♦ In what ways did Paul spell out the freedom Christians have because of Jesus?

♦ What about Paul's words challenges the way you have thought about the law, forgiveness and freedom in the past?

♦ How do Paul's words affect the way you will approach God about your sins in the future?

Paul's words remind us today that we have been set free of the rigid laws the people of the Old Testament were required to keep. We can receive forgiveness anytime and anyplace from Jesus.

I Sure Clean Up Nicely

Because you've been blessed to be alive when the Old Testament rituals of sacrifice and cleansing have been abolished, you have the opportunity to become a new creation in Christ. What does that mean? It means that when you turn your life over to Jesus and ask for forgiveness of your sins, the way you used to be is no longer the way you are.

Before you knew Jesus, you did things God considers sin. Now that you know Jesus, you'll still sin from time to time, but your intention and goal is to do the things which please God instead of yourself. God comes into your

Ask students to take responsibilities for activities in coming weeks. They will rise to the challenge and feel your respect and trust.

Make prayer a priority. Use the time before students arrive to pray in the areas where they will be doing activities, worshiping, praying and discussing.

The law: A foundation for freedom.

life and changes you, if you let Him, and you are never the same. Paul talks about this in 2 Corinthians 5:17. *(Read the verse to the class. Ask volunteers to share with the rest of the class what is different about their lives since they have become Christians. If there are no personal examples shared, ask students to share changes they have seen in other people who have become Christians.)* So, we're new creations when we come to Christ. That means we don't fall into the same sins over and over again because we can be forgiven easily. That would be taking God's incredible gift of salvation lightly.

Now that we're all cleaned up, there are things God wants us to do and certain responsibilities we all share. *(Have students read Eph. 2:10 and 4:24 in their Bibles.)*

♦ What are our lives supposed to be like when we become new creations?

♦ What are we supposed to be doing?

♦ Do you think a person can truly be a new creation because of Jesus and not have holiness and goodness in his life? Why?

♦ In light of today's lesson and the passages we just read, what are some areas of your life where you feel like you would like to be more of a new creation than you have been in the past?

Conclusion

Each of us would be a total failure if God were judging us on how well we have kept the laws of the Old Testament. We don't even know all of the laws from that time, so I'm sure we have broken many of them by now. The laws of the Old Testament show us how desperately we need Jesus to forgive us our sins. Without Jesus, our lives would be full of the rituals and sacrifices we talked about earlier. Because of Christ, we can have meaningful, free relationships with the Lord.

Our Power Point today, *The law: A foundation for freedom*, reminds us that we are no longer under the law, but are free to live as new creations in Christ. Each of us has been given the opportunity to respond to God and be set free from sin and the law. Please pray with me as we close. If you have not asked the Lord for forgiveness of your sins or asked Him to be the Lord of your life, you can do so while I pray or you can see me after class and we can pray together then. Remember, nothing compares to knowing that you are right with God and are in a relationship with Him for now and all eternity.

Dear Lord, thank You for giving us the freedom to receive Your love and forgiveness because of Jesus. We are thankful for the laws of the Old Testament because in light of them, we see our great need for You. We want to be the new creations You desire. Help us by the power of Your Holy Spirit to live holy lives, doing the works You have planned for us. In Jesus' name, amen.

Materials: Construction paper, wrapping (or tissue) paper, ribbon, glue, glitter, scissors, pens and Bibles.

Our Memory Verse is such an important verse in the Bible because it explains the reason God had to send Jesus to die on the cross. If we could follow all the laws in the Old Testament and earn our way to heaven, Jesus would not have needed to die on the cross. But God knows we are sinners and we can never be good enough or holy enough to make it to heaven on our own. So He gave us the most awesome gift we could ever receive—Jesus!

Give the students the construction paper, wrapping paper, ribbon, glue, scissors, pens and glitter. Instruct them to cut out a card in the shape of a present. They can decorate the cover with the supplies to make it look like a gift. On the inside flaps of the card, students should write the following: Flap 1: "God sent His Son to die for my sins." Flap 2: This week's Memory Verse.

After the students have copied the verse onto their cards, encourage them to take a few minutes to commit the verse to memory.

The way sins were forgiven in the Old Testament was different from how we are forgiven today.

♦ **How were people in the Old Testament cleansed and forgiven of their sins?**
Through blood sacrifice.

♦ **How are we cleansed and forgiven of our sins?**

Divide the class into three groups. Read one of the following situations to each group. Ask them to discuss the problem and come up with a solution to offer the person in the situation:

◊ Your friend wants to talk about a problem. She's feeling pretty bad because she took some money from her mom's purse without asking.

◊ Your friend confides in you that he cheated on his final exam in math. He is afraid to confess, but it is tearing him up inside.

◊ Your friend comes to your house with a cut on his head and scrapes on his arm. After asking what happened, he hesitatingly tells you that he took a corner too fast on his bike and hit a parked car. He knew his parents would be really upset, so he panicked and quickly ran away from the scene.

After the students share their responses with the class, discuss the following questions:

♦ **What do all three situations have in common?**

♦ **What was similar about the advice given in all three situations?**

♦ **What advice would God have given to each of these kids?**

♦ **Will God forgive all of these sins?**

Galatians 2:21

This gift is from God, and it is very important to me. If the law could make us right with God, then Christ did not have to die.

The law: A foundation for freedom.

1—Game

Materials: Paper, Bibles, concordance and pencils.

Life in Old Testament times was a lot different from life as we know it today, especially in terms of the way we receive forgiveness for our sins. There were all kinds of sacrifices, rituals and ordinances the people of the Old Testament had to do to be cleansed of their sins.

Have the students get into groups of two or three. Give groups a preset amount of time to look for sacrifices made in the Old Testament. Each group will list the sacrifices and Scripture references they find. After the allotted time, they will create two or three fake sacrifices and references in hopes of stumping the other groups. Have each group read their list to the other groups. After each sacrifice is read, the other teams will vote as to whether or not it is a fake sacrifice or one from the Bible. The team who stumps the other teams is the winner.

2—Creative Writing

Materials: *Club 56 Activity Zone* page 13, Bibles and pencils.

The end result of the sacrifices made in the Old Testament was forgiveness and cleansing from sin. The same goes with asking God directly because of Jesus' sacrifice. I'm going to ask you to put yourself in the shoes of a person from the Old Testament and a person from the New Testament. Think about what each of them may have felt after receiving forgiveness from God. Illustrate how each might have felt from their perspective. You do not need to include why the person needed forgiveness, but you may elect to include details of what they did to receive their cleansing from God. Give the students time to work, then if they feel comfortable, have them share their entries with the rest of the class.

3—Outreach Project

Materials: *Club 56 Activity Zone* page 14, pencils and envelopes.

Each of us has had the opportunity to have God forgive us of our sins through His Son, Jesus. We know we can talk to Him anytime and anyplace. There are some people who don't know this. The other Sunday School teachers in our church do their best to help the children in their classes understand that Jesus is the way we can find forgiveness from God. Sometimes children look at the young people who are just a little older than they are for answers. I think that after this lesson, each of you can tell these young children about God's offer of forgiveness.

Today we will be writing letters to the children in a Sunday School class who are just a little younger than we are. These kids really look up to you, and taking time to write to them may make a big difference in their lives. As our outreach project for this week, let's fill in our activity pages by sharing with them an experience from our own lives when God forgave us.

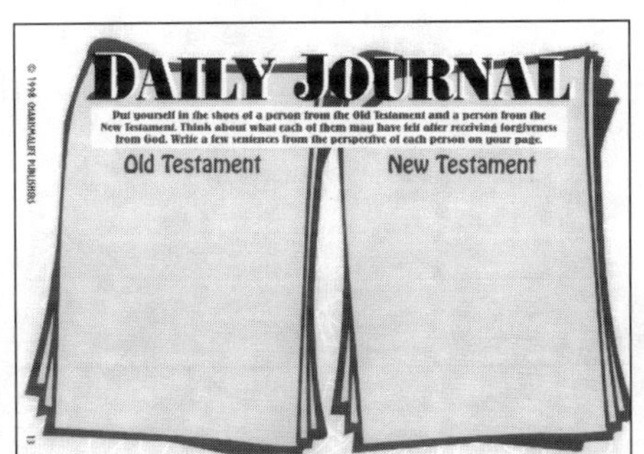

Activity Zone page 13

Activity Zone page 14

Give the students time to fill in the blanks with information from an experience in their own lives. Place the letters in envelopes and deliver them to another classroom. The envelopes do not need to be addressed to specific children in the other class.

4—Object Lesson

Materials: Twine (heavy, 7 strands, 6 feet each), index cards (14), tape, pen and cans of food (14, large).

Before class: Write one of the following Old Testament laws on each index card:

1. Do not eat meat with blood still in it.
2. Do not cut the hair off the sides of your head.
3. Stand when an older person enters the room.
4. When you plant a tree, do not eat its fruit for four years.
5. When you sacrifice an offering, eat it during the first two days.
6. Do not harvest the edges of your field.
7. Do not pick up grapes that have fallen in your vineyard.
8. Do not wait to pay a man until the next day.
9. Do not plant your field with two kinds of seeds.
10. Do not wear clothes made of two kinds of materials.
11. Do not trim your beard.
12. Do not put tattoo marks on yourselves.
13. Keep all the decrees and laws.
14. The High Priest must not uncover his head. (Taken from Leviticus)

Next, tie each end of each strand of twine around a can of food. On each can, tape one index card. Thus, you will have seven strands with one can and one law on each end of the strand.

In our lesson, we compared the laws of the Old Testament to the freedom we now have through Christ. There were over 600 laws in the Old Testament that the Jewish people felt they had to uphold. These laws were written on prayer shawls worn around their necks. These shawls served as a reminder of the laws that had to be kept.

Call a volunteer to the front of the class. Hold up one of the strands of twine and read to the group the two Old Testament laws taped to the cans. Then, place the twine over the volunteer's shoulders. Next, read two more of the laws and place weighted strand over the student's shoulders. Continue with each set of laws until the student feels weighed down by all the laws on his shoulders. It is important that you put enough weights on to illustrate the point that, under the law, we are weighed down with rules and regulations that we will not be able to uphold always. Yet it is extremely important to be careful not to put too much weight onto the student's shoulders to the point of real discomfort.

Call your Sunday School administrator and co—teachers this week to encourage them for the work they do. Don't ask them any questions about the classroom or make any requests of them, just let them know you are thankful for their involvement.

The law: A foundation for freedom.

Discuss the following questions:

♦ How did it feel to have the weights on your shoulders?

♦ How are the weights like the laws in the Old Testament?

♦ We only used 14 laws. How would it feel to have 600 weights? How would it feel to try to uphold 600 laws?

♦ Could you always keep all 600 laws?

♦ What did God do for us since He knew we couldn't keep all of the commands?

Materials: Copies of Living It Out story.

Hi, I'm Lucy Lee Craig. I really need to understand some things so I can make a decision. My brother has been taking me to church for a few months, and I have been hearing about Jesus and how He died to save us. I think that's really neat, but I haven't been able to see how that has anything to do with me. I'm a good person most of the time. Unless you count the times I'm a little cranky. Well, I do lose my temper once in awhile, and I do lie occasionally in an emergency. But other than that, I'm all right. I just can't see why I need a Savior.

I thought I had this all figured out until last Sunday. My little sister, Meg, went into my room and broke my CD player. When I told my mom she just said she was sorry, but I should have kept my door shut. I was furious that she didn't do anything other than tell my sister to stay out of my room.

I went into my room and slammed the door. I sat down on my bed and thought some awful thoughts about my whole family. I'm not even going to tell you what they were because they were so ugly. I didn't know that I could be so terrible. I felt really guilty and sad. Maybe I do need to be a new person.

Today in church I really listened to the pastor. I wanted to know Jesus like the other people who were there. When I hear my Sunday School teacher talk or the pastor speak, Jesus seems like a real person.

In fact, when he asked if anyone wanted to be a Christian it was all I could to keep my hand down. Has that ever happened to you?

Our pastor said everyone has to become a new creature. I'm not sure how that happens. Does it make sense to you? If it does, will you explain it so I can understand? I would really appreciate it. Talk to you later.

©1998 CharismaLife Publishers. Permission is granted to reproduce this story — not for resale.

Can you help Lucy accept Christ?

Divide the class into small discussion groups. Give each group a copy of the Living It Out story. Ask each group to identify the most important questions Lucy was asking and answer them. Conclude the time with a discussion of their answers in the large group setting.

 **Materials:** Copies of Lesson 7 Secret Orders.

You know, this espionage game is a tough one. There are so many things you have to learn, secret codes you have to memorize and regulations you have to follow. I mean, you sure wouldn't want to be the only undercover guy caught without an official overcoat. The thing is, as long as you follow the rules, you will come out of every mission in good shape.

So here is your assignment for the week. Think about all of the different rules you are required to obey—both at home and at school. Record three of the most important rules. Tell why they are important and how they help you in your life.

Remember to bring your completed Secret Orders to class next week.

The law: A foundation for freedom.

Take an inventory of the academic interests of your students. Find out where their strengths lie. Involve activities in your lessons which appeal to these interests and watch your class time become more enjoyable.

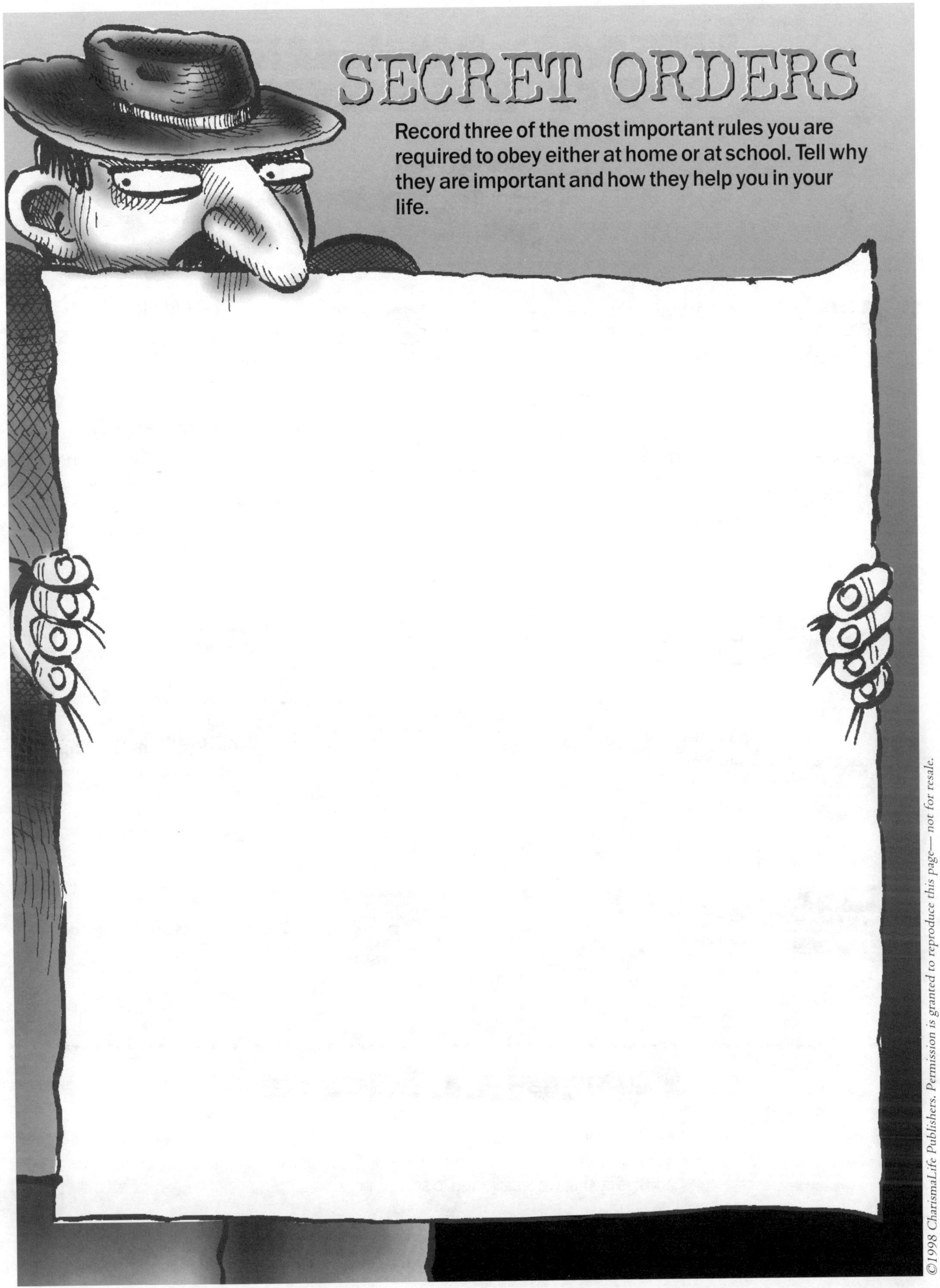

SECRET ORDERS
Record three of the most important rules you are required to obey either at home or at school. Tell why they are important and how they help you in your life.

ITEMS NEEDED FOR LESSON

- ❏ Challenge notebooks
- ❏ Lesson 7 Secret Orders
- ❏ Chalkboard
- ❏ Chalk

- ❏ Peanut butter cups
- ❏ Chalkboard
- ❏ Chalk
- ❏ Napkins

- ❏ Bibles
- ❏ Chalkboard
- ❏ Chalk

- ❏ Posterboard
- ❏ Paper
- ❏ Tape
- ❏ Felt-tip pens
- ❏ Bibles

- ❏ Paper
- ❏ Pencils

1—Individual Art

- ❏ *Club 56 Activity Zone* page 15
- ❏ Markers
- ❏ Tape

2—Object Lesson

- ❏ *Club 56 Activity Zone* page 16
- ❏ Pencils
- ❏ Objects used to hold things together (staples, paper clips, rubber bands, yarn, glue, clothespins and buttons)

3—Game

- ❏ Paper
- ❏ Pencils
- ❏ Small prizes (several)
- ❏ Watch with second hand

4—Problem Solving

- ❏ Chalkboard
- ❏ Chalk

- ❏ Copies of Lesson 8 Secret Orders

SPECIAL NOTE

Many people are constantly trying to live up to God's standard. Help your students realize it is by God's grace and mercy that we are allowed to serve Him.

God can make a way.

My brothers, God called you to be free. But do not use your freedom as an excuse to do the things that please your sinful self. Serve each other with love.

Galatians 5:13

Romans 3:23-24; 2 Corinthians 3:18; Galatians 1:4; 3:10,21-22; 6:9-10; Philippians 1:6

A. Welcome to the Crowd

B. Stinkin' Thinkin'

C. The Divine Way of Doing Things

GOD'S WAYS CAN BE ACCOMPLISHED

"If it can be thought of, it can be done," is one of my husband's favorite sayings. He points to men like Alexander Graham Bell, the Wright brothers and Thomas Edison as examples. Always a dreamer and thinker, Mike has plans and visions for his life that he is convinced can be accomplished because he has dared to imagine them. I admire his boldness and confidence. He believes all things are possible and with Christ's help, probable.

When looking at our imperfections and sin in light of God's holiness and perfection, it is easy to feel like we will never be able to measure up or to please God. Although "measuring up" is not what God had in mind when He created us, He does desire that we please Him. What is the easiest way to please Him? Do His will, follow His commands and accomplish what He has set out for us to do. The Holy Spirit is the Enabler who will help us to do these seemingly impossible and often overwhelming tasks. Through God's grace, Christ's redemption and the Holy Spirit's power, we can be changed, we can grow and we can pursue God.

Encourage the students in your class that they can please God. His will and ways can be accomplished in their lives, not because they are without sin and able to keep God's laws to the letter, but because Christ in them is the hope of glory. The power of the Holy Spirit operating in their lives equips them to overcome sin and finish the race with strength. God has set His will and plans before us. His ways can be accomplished. If it can be thought of, with His help it can be done.

Materials: Challenge notebooks, Lesson 7 Secret Orders, chalkboard and chalk.

Take time to go over the three rules each person decided were most important to them. List the ones the class thinks are most important on the chalkboard. Discuss with your class why they think they are the most important.

Have the students place their completed Secret Orders in their Challenge notebooks.

Materials: Peanut butter cups, chalkboard, chalk and napkins.

Note: Be sure you have enough peanut butter cups for each student to receive one.

There's a commercial for a certain kind of candy that highlights the different ways the candy can be eaten and claims there is really no wrong way to do it. We are going to see how many ways we can come up with to eat peanut butter cups.

Make a list on the chalkboard of the different options students recommend. Suggestions might include: Chewing the ridges off around the outside first, breaking it in half and eating the peanut butter part first, regular bites, poking the middle out and eating it first, etc. Let the students vote on which responses are the funniest, grossest, most creative and most boring. Hand out the peanut butter cups and napkins and allow the students to eat them however they choose.

Although there were no wrong ways to eat your peanut butter cups today, there are things in life that are supposed to be done or handled in one right or correct way. Today we will be talking about accomplishing God's ways in the ways He intends for them to be accomplished.

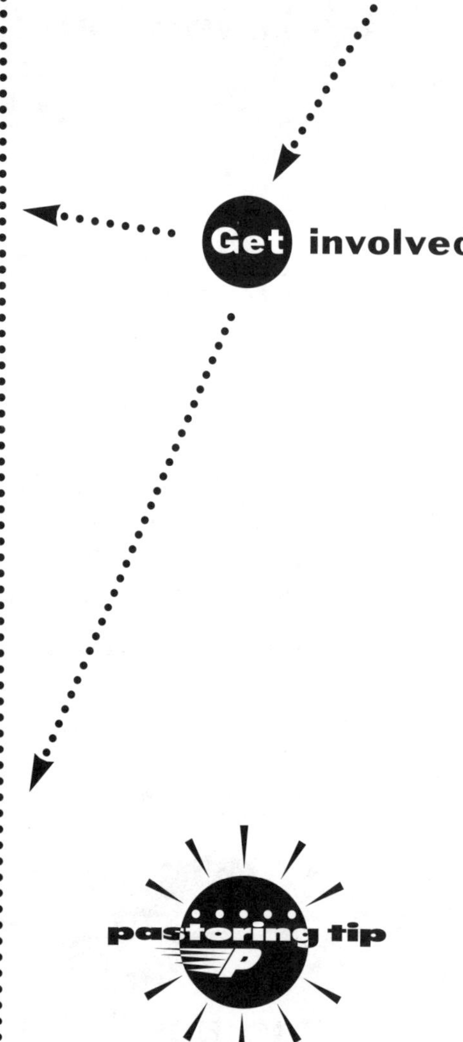

God can make a way in your life today. As you face obstacles in your teaching, trust the Lord to carry you through.

God can make a way.

Materials: Bibles, chalkboard and chalk.

Welcome to the Crowd

By now I think most of us realize that no one is perfect. We all make mistakes—even though some of them are accidental—and undoubtedly we all sin. There is not a single person in this room who has never sinned. Remember, sin isn't just the big stuff like murder and robbery. Sin is anything we do which God says is wrong. God says lying is wrong. Gossiping is wrong. Mistreating others is wrong. At one time or another we've all blown it with one of these things. *(Have a student read Rom. 3:23 at this point).*

We also know there is a pretty steep penalty that goes along with sinning. You'll experience things here on earth that will be difficult and painful because of sin, but there is an even greater price we all should pay in terms of God.

♦ **What are some of the ways we may "pay" for our sins (like lying, gossiping or mistreating people) here on earth?** *We may lose friends; get in trouble with our parents; lose people's trust; get treated wrongly in return, etc.*

♦ **What is the price we should pay with God because of our sins?**

Many people think the ultimate price for sinning is going to hell. The thing I want you to understand is that hell is a real place and that is where unbelievers will spend eternity. The worst thing about hell is that it is so far away from God. The great punishment for our sins is that we are cut off from a relationship with God and have to live separately. The only way to be freed from that kind of separation and distance is to have forgiveness from God.

Fortunately, we can all turn to Him and receive that forgiveness. Everyone in this room and in the entire world can ask God to free them from sin. God's Word tells us this, so we can believe it. *(Have a student read Rom. 3:24).*

It sounds like we have a lot of common ground with each other, doesn't it? We all sin, and we all need God to set us free from sin. From the lessons we have already covered in our classes together, we also share a common belief as to how we are able to receive God's forgiveness and why. We base our entire faith on our relationship with God made possible through Jesus Christ's death and resurrection. He died for our sins so we wouldn't have to be separated from God. In the days when Paul was writing to the people in Galatia, there was an additional way being taught as a way to get to God. Paul made a point of teaching that this other way was not what God intended.

Stinkin' Thinkin'

Many of the first people to believe in Jesus were Jewish converts. They had a lot of concerns about how they were supposed to live their lives now that they were Christians. You see, as Jews, they were taught to keep many laws in order to be right with God. As Christians, they were made right with God through Christ and were freed from the strictness of their earlier laws.

This also made them have questions about how people who had not lived their lives as Jews would be able to be called Christians. Some of the Jews taught that Gentile Christians (people who became Christians who had not been Jewish) should have to keep the original Jewish laws as well as accept Christ in order to be accepted by God.

Paul believed God had called him to share his faith with the non-Jewish people of the world, so he felt it was vitally important that he clear this matter up and make sure things were on track again. He knew that if people made keeping the law as important as accepting Christ, it could potentially damage the freedom Jesus had purchased and the Holy Spirit promotes. Let's take a look at a few of the words Paul wrote to explain this.

(Have the students get into three groups. Assign each group one of the following verses: Gal. 1:4; 3:10 and 3: 21-22. Have each group read their verses looking for the answers to the following questions: What does the Scripture say about the law? What does the Scripture say about the people who try to follow the law? What does the Scripture say about the alternative to the law? In some cases all three questions may be answered in a passage. Suggested answers follow.

Galatians 1:4 – *Jesus died for our sins to free us from this evil world.*

Galatians 3:10 – *You can't depend on being able to follow the law. There is a curse for those who cannot follow it.*

Galatians 3:21-22 – *The law isn't against God's promises, but it is given so people will see their need for Jesus in light of how difficult it is to keep.*

Have the groups share their findings with the rest of the class. Record their answers on the chalkboard.)

Paul said even more to convince the people that being right with God is about being forgiven of our sins, not keeping the law so perfectly that sin is impossible. Sin is very possible. You and I know it firsthand. That's why it's so important that Paul took the time to set the people straight.

The Divine Way of Doing Things

So if we are made right with God because of our faith in Him and His willingness to forgive us based on that faith, does that mean it's cool to spend the rest of our lives sinning and asking God to forgive us, sinning again and asking God to forgive us again and sinning some more? No way. God wants us to follow Him and He wants us to follow His ways. The way He wants us to do it is the important thing. He wants us to accomplish His ways by looking to Him to help us do it rather than trying to do it on our own.

God wants us to overcome sin. He sets the plans in motion to make it possible. Remember what we heard about in Galatians 1:4? *(Have the group who reported on this verse share it with the class.)*

Jesus is the major part of God's plan to help us follow His ways. He also sent us the Holy Spirit to support us and help us make right choices. God wants us to love, serve and care for each other. He wants us to grow and mature as Christians to let others know about God's mercy because of the lives we lead. He wants us to hold onto the freedom Jesus gave His life for and not get wrapped up and held down by sin all over again.

Celebrate with your class. When a big event happens in one of the lives of your students, give her attention and invite the rest of the class to join in.

God can make a way.

There are loads of verses in the Bible written to encourage believers not to give up or quit pursuing God's ways. We can accomplish His ways when we go about doing them His way. Let's take a look at a few of those verses and see how they relate to the life of a 5th or 6th grader. *(Have the students get into the same three groups as earlier in the lesson. Assign each group one of the following verses: 2 Cor. 3:18; Phi. 1:6 and Gal. 6:9-10. Have the groups read their verses and decide on one situation in which the verse might give encouragement to a 5th or 6th grader. Have the groups share their answers with the rest of the class.)*

Conclusion

When you feel like you'll never be perfect or be able to measure up to all the laws in the Bible, instead of giving up or feeling rotten, turn to God and thank Him. Thank Him that He knows you so well He has taken care of your needs and concerns, weaknesses and inadequacies. He is there for you, willing to help you by the power of His Holy Spirit to be and do all that He wants so that His ways are accomplished.

Remind yourself of the verses we just read and today's Power Point—*God can make a way.* He knows you, your needs and the plans He has for your life. Let's talk to Him today.

Dear Lord, we are thankful we can call You Father. You have made a way for us to be Your sons and daughters, and we are so thankful. Thank You for not running out of room in Your heart or Your plans for each of us. You are a good and loving Father, and we want to know better how to be Your children. Thank You for helping us to overcome sin in our lives. We love You. In Jesus' name, amen.

Encourage your students to reach out to visitors. Ask the student leaders in your class to welcome new students and familiarize them with your classroom set up and schedule.

Galatians 5:13

My brothers, God called you to be free. But do not use your freedom as an excuse to do the things that please your sinful self. Serve each other with love.

Materials: Posterboard, paper, tape, felt-tip pens and Bibles.

Before class: At the top of a large sheet of posterboard, write this week's Memory Verse. Then tape a piece of paper over the verse so it cannot be seen. Next make three columns on the chart. Label the columns "Verses," "People Served" and "Services." Then list the following Scripture in the Verses column: John 13:1-17, Luke 5:17-26, Luke 9:10-17 and John 2:1-11. Tape the poster to the wall.

In our Memory Verse we are reminded that if we have a relationship with Christ, we are free from the laws and rules of the Old Testament. Jesus fulfilled the law by His death. But we are also reminded that, although we have this freedom, we are not to use it as an excuse to sin. Instead, our verse tells us to serve others. Let's take a minute to memorize our verse.

Give the students time to look up the Memory Verse and memorize it. When students think they have it memorized, ask them to stand by the chart, recite the verse from memory and then lift the flap to see if they said it correctly. When all of the students have successfully memorized the verse, take the flap off the chart.

In our Memory Verse, we are told to serve each other with love. We can look at the life of Jesus for examples of how to serve other people. Let's take a look at a few of these examples.

Divide the students into four groups. Assign each group one of the passages listed on the chart. Ask them to read and discuss the passage as a group and then choose a volunteer to fill in the chart. When all of the groups have finished, ask for each group to share with the class about their passage.

1—Individual Art

Materials: *Club 56 Activity Zone* page 15, markers and tape.

Road signs help guide drivers as they maneuver their cars along highways and streets. What are some of the more common signs you have seen on the road? *Allow the students to respond to the question with as many signs as they can identify.* When people disregard or ignore signs, there are often dangerous consequences. We've learned today that it is important to follow God's laws for many reasons, one of which is the consequences which may arise if we don't.

Imagine for a moment that you have been assigned to create a road sign of sorts to alert people to what may happen if they don't follow God's ways. What symbols or artwork would you use on your sign? Now imagine your assignment is to create a sign to serve as a guideline to tell people how to follow God's ways. Take a moment to think of what this sign would look like.

Hand out the activity pages. **Use your page to illustrate the sign which would be the most convincing in terms of getting people to follow God's ways. The signs can be signs of warning, direction or information.**

Allow the students time to work, then have them tell about their signs.

2—Object Lesson

Materials: *Club 56 Activity Zone* page 16, pencils and objects used to hold things together (staples, paper clips, rubber bands, yarn, glue, clothespins and buttons).

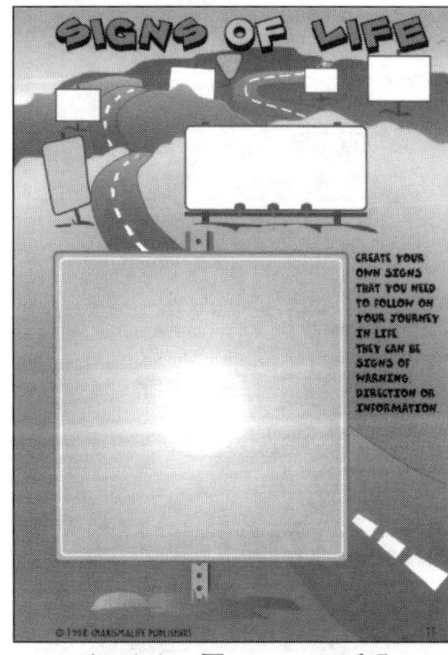

Activity Zone page 15

Activity Zone page 16

God can make a way.

We've spent a lot of time talking about the combination of law and freedom which helps us to be the Christians God is looking for. We've also learned that it is the power of the Holy Spirit that helps us to overcome sin and follow God's ways. Consider for a moment how you would teach this same lesson to a group of third graders. They might not understand everything you were able to catch because you're 5th and 6th graders. You would need to break down the lesson and simplify it. Guess what? That's what you're going to do now.

Display the items from the list of materials. These common objects help hold things together. They may attach two pieces of paper or fabric. They may even make permanent connections. Your task is to find the object you like best and describe how it is like the Holy Spirit who helps us make the connection between the law of the Old Testament and the freedom Jesus gives.

Write your explanation on your page. Remember to keep it simple—you're writing for third graders! Have the students present what they have written as an object lesson for the rest of the class.

3—Game

Materials: Paper, pencils, small prizes (several) and watch with second hand.

One of the points we covered today is that we all are sinners. We all are in need of God's forgiveness if we are going to make it in this world and spend eternity with Him. It helps to know the Holy Spirit is with us to give us strength as we do good and follow God's ways. Having friends with whom we have things in common, like a relationship with the Lord, can also help and give us the support we need.

Today we are going to take a closer look at each other—especially the people in the class we don't know very well. Have the students get into pairs. Encourage the students to choose partners with whom they rarely work. Have the students write down the things they have in common. Award the prizes to the pair(s) with the most things in common according to their lists.

4—Problem Solving

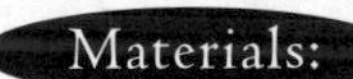
Materials: Chalkboard and chalk.

It is often said that to be truly great at anything, you need the support of those around you. If you wanted to be an Olympic gymnast or a rock star, you wouldn't be able to do it on your own. You would need the support of others.

♦ What are some kinds of support you would need? *Financial support for lessons and training, encouragement, coaching, etc.*

The Holy Spirit promises us that He will give us support in our lives. The Holy Spirit will help us to overcome sin. We know He will give us support, but what does that really mean? How will He support us and help us?

Ask the students to get into groups of three. I am going to read a story to you. I want your group to come up with at least three ways the Holy Spirit would give support to help the character overcome sin.

Read the following paragraph aloud: **Tom seems to be the most popular kid in school. He is quick with a joke and always ready for any adventure, but Tom has a real problem. He lies all the time. He knows it's wrong and even promises himself that he will stop. But when other people are around, he finds himself trying to impress them with his made-up stories. Sometimes, he even lies for no reason. He gets discouraged because he feels like there is no hope for him.**

♦ How will the Holy Spirit give him support to overcome his sin? *Bible, prayer, godly counsel, conscience, etc.*

When all of the groups have finished discussing, ask for volunteers to share their responses. Then make a list of all the ways the Holy Spirit might give support. Have the students call out responses as you write them on the chalkboard.

Materials: Paper and pencils.

Hi, I'm David L. Washington, and I'm in a lot of trouble! I suppose you want to know the whole ugly story, don't you?

I haven't even told my best friend the truth yet. I wish I could do last Thursday all over again. Then maybe I would make a better decision than the one I made. OK, get to the point, right?

I told my teacher a lie about why my homework wasn't ready. I said that I was busy taking care of my mom because she had pneumonia. I told her that my little sister got sick, too, and I just didn't have time. The more I talked the bigger my story got. I couldn't seem to stop.

I don't want to be a liar! The problem is that every time I get into a tough situation, I lie. Even when I say to myself that I will never lie again as long as I live.

It's scary for me! My dad said that if I keep lying about stuff all the time pretty soon no one will believe anything I say. I don't want that to happen to me. There's this girl at school—everyone makes fun of her because she lies and brags all the time. We all know the stories she tells aren't true, but I don't think she knows we know. I don't want to be like that.

When you tell lies you always have to have another lie ready in case someone finds out. It can be pretty tiring sometimes!

Would you be surprised if I tell you that I am a Christian? Well, I am. My mom says that Jesus will help me, but I don't know what to do.

When I got home today there was a message on the answering machine from my teacher. She said that she is going to call our house later tonight to check on my mom. And now my teacher is going to know that I'm a liar, unless I lie again. I don't want her to not trust me anymore. What can I do?

Can you help me? I want to know if Jesus really can help me. Will you talk this over and let me know? Thanks.

God can make a way.

Change the "where" and "how" you teach from time to time. Teach sitting if you usually stand. Teach from the side of the room instead of from the front. This will get the students to pay closer attention to what you are saying and allow you to break the monotony in your lessons.

Can you help David?

Divide the class into small discussion groups. Have each group discuss the questions below and then write a letter to David answering his questions.

♦ Why did David lie about his homework?

♦ Why does David's lying frighten him?

♦ Why does one sin lead to another?

Materials: Copies of Lesson 8 Secret Orders.

Not every mission we go on can be a success. As terrible as it feels, we all have those files where things didn't go as they should. The great thing to remember is that the Big Boss doesn't hold on to those failure files. Instead, He removes them from our permanent record so that it won't affect things we want to do in the future.

Another cool thing the Big Boss does for us is to keep His promises. I mean, I have never, not even once, seen the Big Guy not come through. He can always make a way.

Your assignment for this week is to come up with two promises that God has already made to you—either personally or in the Bible. Write these down and bring them to class next week. Let's hear about some of the awesome things we can look forward to with confidence.

Remember to bring your completed Secret Orders to class next week.

SECRET ORDERS

Come up with two promises that God has already made to you either personally or in the Bible. Write them down and bring them to class next week.

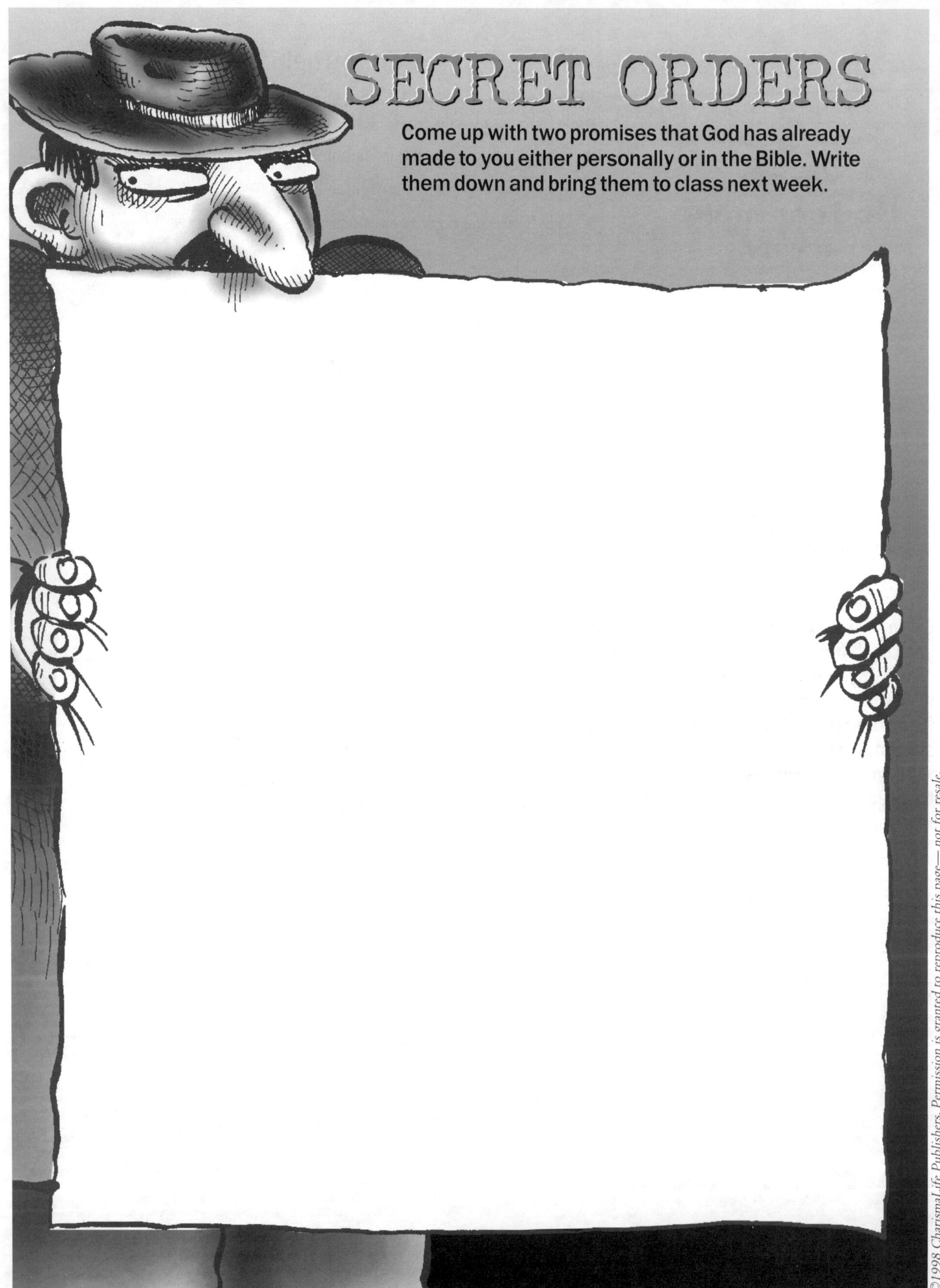

Want to see your team fired up and equipped to minister more effectively?

Consider hosting an information-packed one-day teacher training seminar.
We have two conference programs to serve you:

For Youth Workers

A one-day, hands-on, practical day of training, fellowship and vision impartation for youth leaders and workers in your area that will include two general sessions, four workshops, LIVE! Cross Training session and complimentary luncheon.

For Children's Workers

A one-day conference for Sunday School and Children's Ministry workers who teach preschool - 6th grades that includes two general sessions, four workshops, two LIVE! classroom demonstrations and a complimentary luncheon.

It's easy to be a host church:

▌ Tell us when...

Give us a few dates that are convenient for you. Our conferences typically take place on a Saturday.

▌ We provide the trainers...

We'll send CharismaLife ministry consultants to put on a dynamic program that will give your team a heart full of hope and a handful of practical help.

▌ Give your team the training they need to succeed...

These affordable full-day conferences are a MUST for anyone who desires to minister more effectively to children and teens. You'll receive a wealth of hands-on techniques. Be a blessing and on the cutting edge of ministry by being a host church.

▌ We tell you what to do...

We'll send you a simple and clear information packet that outlines the advantages of hosting a regional conference _and_ tell you what you can expect from us!

▌ Here's what others have said...

"Hosting the CharismaLife Regional Conference was an enjoyable and rewarding time for us. The instructors were able to impart a fresh vision into our local teachers and workers. I recommend this conference to anyone."

Johnny R. Green
Spring Tabernacle — Spring, TX

"I am still getting calls from churches thanking us for hosting the event. We thank you for allowing us to host this event."

Debra Scott
Northwest Church — Federal Way, WA

For a detailed listing of seminar content and free Host Church information packet, call

1-800-451-4598
Ext. 7801

600 Rinehart Road ● Lake Mary, FL 32746 ● www.CharismaLife.com

Sponsored by

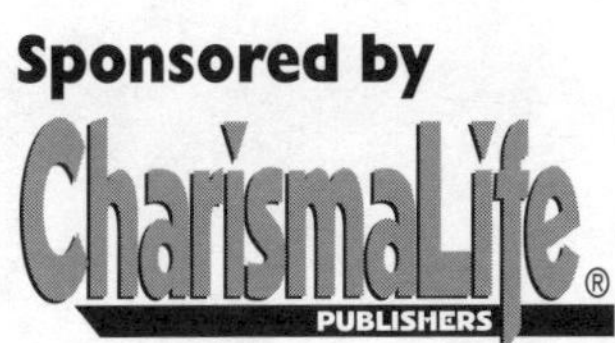

ITEMS NEEDED FOR LESSON

- ❏ Challenge notebooks
- ❏ Lesson 8 Secret Orders

- ❏ Magazines
- ❏ Scissors
- ❏ Tape
- ❏ Paper
- ❏ Markers

- ❏ Chalkboard
- ❏ Chalk
- ❏ Scraps of paper
- ❏ Pens

- ❏ *Club 56 Activity Zone* page 17
- ❏ Pencils

- ❏ None

1—Game

- ❏ Chalkboard
- ❏ Chalk
- ❏ Dice
- ❏ Tootsie Rolls (small)

2—Creative Writing

- ❏ Paper
- ❏ Pencils

3—Cooking

- ❏ Cookie sheet (small)
- ❏ Knife
- ❏ Pot holder
- ❏ Plastic wrap
- ❏ Toaster oven
- ❏ Spatula
- ❏ Refrigerated cookie dough with surprise shapes in center (two packages)

4—Group Art

- ❏ *Club 56 Activity Zone* page 18
- ❏ Pens
- ❏ Felt-tip pens

- ❏ Copies of Lesson 9 Secret Orders

SPECIAL NOTE

The Memory Verse activity includes a skit for today's lesson. Take the time to allow your students to be very creative. Skits provide a vehicle for your students to express themselves and how they feel about various subjects.

Relationship with God has its privileges.

So I tell you: Live by following the Spirit. Then you will not do what your sinful selves want.

Galatians 5:16

Galatians 2:20; 3:13-14

A. It's Changed My Life!

B. And That's Not All! If You Act Now...

C. Operators Are Standing By

BENEFITS OF THE SPIRIT-LED LIFE

I love wholesale shopping. Though I rarely need three loaves of bread, ten gallons of dish washing detergent or 48 rolls of toilet paper, I find myself putting them in my cart because of the great deals I get as a member of our local wholesale club. It's not just that the prices are supposed to be better at bulk stores or that the entire shopping experience is reminiscent of walking through a behind-the-scenes warehouse, it's more the fact that I am part of a club not open to the general public. I have always loved clubs—girls' clubs, church clubs, school clubs, women's clubs—you name it, I have joined. I love membership cards, special patches, meetings and belonging.

In one way or another, we are all like that. We want to be a part of something important. We want to be a part of something special and unique. Through Jesus, we are all part of a club of sorts. What's unique about Jesus' club is that it is open to everyone. He has already paid the dues, and no renewal notices are sent. There are benefits and rewards for every day we spend on this earth followed by the privilege of spending eternity with the Lord when our days are finished.

Teach the students in your class that the Christian life is about more than getting to heaven. Let them know that their times before heaven can be filled with benefits and blessing because of the relationship they share with the Lord.

Materials: Challenge notebooks and Lesson 8 Secret Orders.

How many of you wrote down two promises that God has already made to you? Let's share them with the rest of the class and see how God is faithful in keeping His promises.

Have the students place their completed Secret Orders in their Challenge notebooks.

Materials: Magazines, scissors, tape, paper and markers.

How many of you have ever watched an infomercial? Sometimes they are so annoying that we flip the channel as soon as we see them, and other times we might actually sit through a few minutes of the advertisements.

♦ What are some of the common characteristics of these programs? *Celebrity endorsements, testimonials, information about ordering, etc.*

One of the things I have found to be a common part of infomercials is the add-on stuff they throw in at the end of the "here's how to order part" to get people to call in and buy the product.

Today we are going to hunt for the same kinds of ads in these magazines. Take a few minutes to work with a partner. Thumb through the magazines and cut out the advertisement you find. Tape the advertising onto a piece of paper and prepare to present it to the rest of the class. In your presentation you will need to tell us about the product, how much it costs and what exactly you get for your money.

Allow time for the students to work, then present their ads to the class. If advertisements are difficult to find, permit the students to create their own illustrations for popular ads they have seen on television.

Today's lesson is about an incredible deal you won't want to pass up. The bonuses with this deal are almost as great as the deal itself. See what you think about the offer you'll receive today.

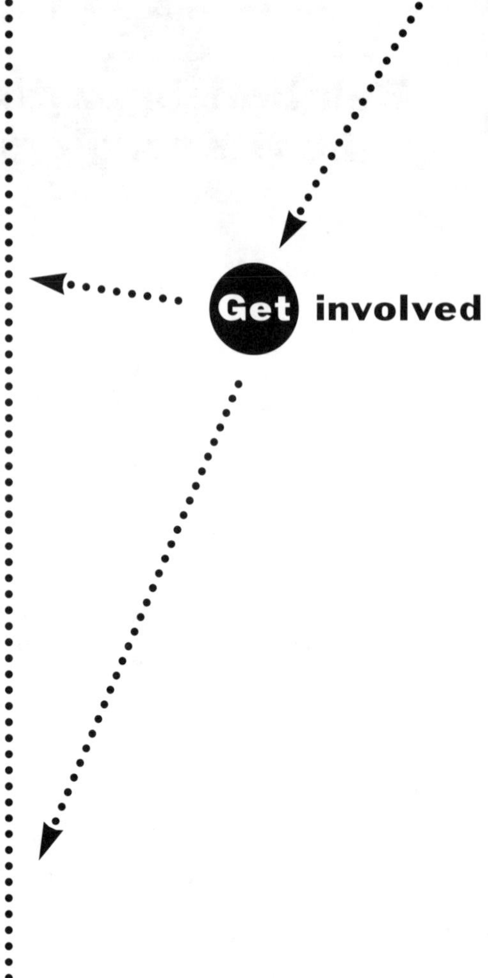

You are a walking testimonial for Christ to your classroom. Let your students see your relationship with the Lord in the way you talk, play, listen and teach.

Relationship with God has its privileges.

Enlist the help of other teachers with activities. No man is an island, and neither is a teacher. The students will respond to different teaching styles and learning will be more effective.

Materials: Chalkboard, chalk, scraps of paper and pens.

It's Changed My Life!

Today we're going to talk about being Christians. I think we do that just about every week, but this time we are going to look at it from a slightly different perspective. Let's imagine you are walking down one of the streets in our city and you decide to do an informal survey of the people you pass. You ask each person what's the best reason for knowing God. Most people would answer with the same words. Do you think you can guess what those words would be? *(Distribute the paper scraps and pens. Have the students print what they think would be the most suggested answer. Several answers may be offered.)* One of the main reasons people think it is good to know God is so they can go to heaven. In fact, some of us may feel that way. After our lesson, I hope you will feel differently.

I know that even if nothing else ever happens to me, knowing God has been a rewarding experience. Would you agree? On the back of your scrap of paper, print one thing from your personal experience that has made being a Christian worthwhile. Keep your answers to yourselves; we'll refer to them later in our lesson.

Galatians 2:20 reminds us of the incredible act Jesus did for us to give us the opportunity to become Christians. The verse tells us about the salvation Jesus gives and the love He has for each of us. *(Have a volunteer read this verse.)*

♦ **What does this verse say about how our lives are different if we have received what Jesus did for us by dying for our sins?** *It says Christ lives in us. We live now by faith.*

You see, salvation doesn't just change where we will spend eternity. It changes who we are and how we live—way before we ever get to heaven.

And That's Not All! If You Act Now...

There's even more. If we read further in Galatians, there is an added bonus we can receive when we accept Jesus as our Savior. *(Have a student read Gal. 3:13-14.)*

♦ **What else did God promise we could receive because Jesus has taken all of our sins upon Himself?** *The Spirit.*

I know we covered this one in previous lessons, so this next question should be review for most of us.

♦ **What are some of the benefits of receiving the Holy Spirit in our lives?** *More power to do God's will; a special prayer language; ability to discern and hear God more clearly, etc.*

Those answers sound more like things we would need while we are here on earth than when we get to heaven. They kind of reinforce the point that God's salvation is for today, not just for when we are dying and facing eternity.

The Bible is loaded with tons of other benefits for our earthly lives. There are privileges which accompany a relationship with God.

♦ **What do you think they are?** *Peace, confidence; hope for the future; having God to talk to; receiving answers for prayers; healing, etc.*

(As students respond, list their answers on the board. When students have exhausted their ideas, have them read the item they wrote on their scraps of paper earlier in the lesson.) Read what you have written and come up with another item for our list. Think about how that experience affected your life and how the event could be summed up as a benefit or privilege which comes from having a relationship with the Lord. *(Give students time to rethink their answers, then add their statements to the list on the board.)*

Think about the infomercials and ads we discussed earlier. I know a relationship with God, the benefits it provides and the gift of eternal life it guarantees are more significant than any product offered during the wee hours of the morning on television, but imagine for a moment that there was an advertisement on television for them. Who do you think would be the spokesperson? What would the infomercial be like? Think you can come up with an idea or two? Here's your chance. *(Have the students get into pairs or small groups to think and plan their infomercials. Allow each group three minutes to present their infomercials.)*

Operators Are Standing By

As a final plug for the products offered on television through infomercials, companies often show before and after photos of the people who have used their products. These people testify to the incredible difference the product has made in their lives. Each of us is a walking advertisement for the gift of salvation made available through Christ.

There are people all around you at school, in your neighborhood, on your sports team, in your church and in your family who are looking at you to see if being a Christian is worth it. They're checking you out to see if the benefits outweigh the sacrifices, if your relationship is real or just put on in front of other people. They want to know if the answers to life's problems are about religion and going to church or a relationship with God.

What do you think they are seeing? What kind of a spokesperson are you? Do people know about the privileges of a relationship with God because of what they see in you? *(Ask the students to recall a time when someone asked them about being a Christian or a time when they shared about Christ with a friend.)*

♦ How did you handle the situation?

♦ How might you handle the situation differently after today's lesson?

♦ How would you have answered the question from our informal poll of people on the street? Would you have mentioned heaven in your answer or the quality of your life here on earth? Why?

The benefits and privileges we've talked about today are available to everyone. If you have been a Christian just so you can go to heaven, think about all the things we've just heard. Let's take a few minutes to talk to the Lord and ask Him to help us get all we can out of being Christians, no matter how long we will be on earth. *(Pause for a moment to allow students time to pray silently, then offer a prayer for the group.)*

Remind students that the benefits and privileges of a relationship with the Lord do not cancel out the fact that everyone will experience tough times and difficulties in life. Help them see that a relationship with the Lord helps and supports us through the rough days.

Relationship with God has its privileges.

Lord, we love You. We want to have a relationship with You for more reasons than just getting to go to heaven. That is a wonderful gift from You, and we are so thankful for it, but today, Lord, we want to thank You for the awesome and incredible things You do in us and for us while we are on earth. You are good to us and are worthy of our thanks. Help us, by Your Holy Spirit, to be more sensitive to the opportunities, benefits and privileges which are ours because we are Yours. We love You. In Jesus' name, amen.

Conclusion

Today can be an incredible day for each of us if we will take the time to think about the ways our lives are different because we have a relationship with the Lord. This may be the first time you have ever really thought of the benefits of following Christ and living a Spirit–led life. God is with you and has great things in store for your todays, tomorrows and eternity. Take time this week to remember our Power Point—*Relationship with God has its privileges.*

Galatians 5:16

So I tell you: Live by following the Spirit. Then you will not do what your sinful selves want.

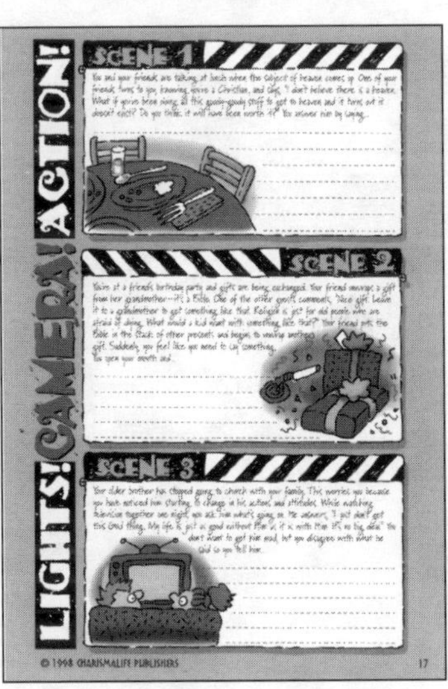

Activity Zone page 17

Materials: *Club 56 Activity Zone* page 17 and pencils.

You will come across lots of people who don't understand the benefits of a personal relationship with Jesus. They may think that being a Christian is just about being good or wanting to go to heaven. We've learned some things today in class which might help you answer their questions or help them understand what a relationship with Jesus is all about.

Have the students read the three scenes from their activity pages with a partner. Next, have the partners work for a few minutes to create a skit for one of the scenes. Students should act out possible reactions, conversation and additional questions which could arise in the scene.

1—Game

Materials: Chalkboard, chalk, dice and Tootsie Rolls (small).

Having a relationship with God has so many awesome benefits. Of course, it ultimately means we will be in heaven. Until then, we will have benefits while we are here on earth! We are going to play a little game to see if you can figure out some of the rewards.

Play the game by using the following directions.

Divide the students into four teams. Position the teams so they can all see the chalkboard.

Choose one of the benefits listed below or one of your own. Instead of writing the words on the board, write dashes, one for each letter. Be sure to leave space between words. For example, the words "eternal life" should be seen as _ _ _ _ _ _ _ _ _ _ _. Examples of benefits include: eternal life, hope for the future, forgiveness of sins, purpose in life, freedom from death and divine healing.

The first team will roll the dice. They will name a letter. If the letter is found in the puzzle, the teacher will write the letter above the corresponding dash and the team will receive the number of Tootsie Rolls as the number rolled on the dice. They will then roll again. They will continue with their turn until they guess a letter that is not in the puzzle. If it is not in the puzzle, the team does not get any Tootsie Rolls. The dice then goes to the next team. The game continues until one team solves the puzzle.

Start a new puzzle and play several rounds. At the end, make sure all the students have at least one candy as a reward for their effort.

2—Creative Writing

Materials: Paper and pencils.

When a person dies, he often leaves a will. A lawyer reads the will to the surviving friends and family to let them know about any inheritance they will receive. There are many things we have inherited from God because of His Son, Jesus. If a lawyer were writing a letter to you to explain the benefits, privileges and inheritance you were in line to receive because of Jesus, what do you think he would say? Use your page to create an official-sounding letter from the law office of Mr. Ben E. Fitts.

Have the students read their letters to the rest of the class when they are finished.

3—Cooking

Materials: Cookie sheet (small), knife, pot holder, plastic wrap, toaster oven, spatula, refrigerated cookie dough with surprise shapes in center (two packages).

Note: Many grocery stores carry cookie dough in the dairy section which has shapes made of contrasting colors in the center of the dough. These shapes are only revealed when the cookies are cut. Choose two packages of this type of cookie dough.

Before class: If your class will not have access to a toaster oven during Sunday School, prepare several cookies from one package of dough beforehand. Otherwise, set aside time in class to make the cookies with the students. If you will be able

Relationship with God has its privileges.

to bake during class time, leave one package of dough wrapped. Unwrap the other package of cookie dough and wrap in the plastic wrap. Bring this dough to class so the students will not know about the design in the center of the dough.

Many people look at Christianity and think it's just about getting to heaven. We know otherwise. Being a Christian is about following God throughout our whole lives. There are benefits and privileges we can experience every day. I think you could say that with Christianity, there is more than meets the eye. There are lots of things in nature that are more than what meets the eye. Can you think of any foods for which this is true?

Now we're going to have a treat which is "more than what meets the eye." Display the plastic-wrapped cookie dough. This looks like a regular roll of cookie dough, doesn't it? Really, it is more than that. This cookie dough reminds me that a relationship with God is about more than just getting to heaven or being a good person. There are hidden blessings and privileges to serving God—like the ones we discovered today.

Cut the cookie dough with the knife to reveal the shape inside the dough. Bake several cookies according to the directions on the package, or serve the cookies you prepared in advance.

4—Group Art

Materials: *Club 56 Activity Zone* page 18, pens and felt-tip pens.

Membership has its privileges. Have you seen the commercials on television using this slogan to advertise a credit card? They tell us that being a member of this company and owning its credit card has special benefits.

♦ What are some benefits or privileges a credit card company could offer? *Buy things; rent cars; take it on trips, etc.*

Our Power Point tells us that a relationship with God has its privileges. Besides giving us eternal life, we are given many benefits here on earth.

♦ What are some of the benefits and privileges a relationship with God can give us?

If you want to apply for a credit card, you are given a brochure that describes all of the qualifications you must meet, the benefits that come with membership and the responsibilities you take on as a card owner. You are going to have the opportunity to work with a small group to design a brochure that lists the qualifications, benefits and responsibilities of having a relationship with God.

Divide the students into small groups. Hand out the activity pages, pens and felt-tip pens. After the groups have completed their brochures, ask them to share them with the class. The brochures can be folded like accordions.

Activity Zone page 18

Phil swung the bat at the ball and grimaced as he missed it once again. "Dick, I'm over here!"

Dick laughed and tossed it again. "Are you feeling OK?" he asked Phil. This was the first time Phil had ventured outside since he got home from the hospital.

"I feel good all the time now, Dick. I told you that Jesus healed me while I was in the hospital."

Dick just tossed the ball in the air. He didn't want to have a disagreement with his friend so soon after he got out of the hospital. After all, Phil almost died. If it wasn't for the miracle of modern science, he wouldn't be here right now.

"Do you know how many people were praying for me?" Phil asked Dick. For some reason he just didn't seem to be able to drop it. He wanted Dick to understand that he had been healed. "Everyone in our church prayed, and then they put my name on prayer chains all over the world. People who didn't know me were praying. Can you believe that?"

Dick decided to say what was on his mind. "I'm really glad that you're better, Phil. I was really worried, but I don't believe all that stuff about God healing you. He doesn't do that kind of thing anymore."

Phil smiled, "Yes, he does, Dick. In fact, while I was really sick, God talked to me. He told me that He loved me and He was going to heal me so I could tell people that He loved them."

Dick sat down on the ground and practiced balancing the ball on his knee. "OK, if God heals, then why didn't He heal all the people in the hospital? See what I mean? You got well because of all the medicine you got, not because God picked you out of a crowd and healed you."

Phil didn't know what to say. Maybe he'd been too hasty about telling people God healed him. Phil nodded to Dick and said he needed to get home. They got on their bikes and headed in opposite directions.

As he hopped off his bike at home, his friend Gary leaped over the fence from his yard. "Hi, how are you doing? My mom said that it's a real miracle that you are home."

Phil wasn't sure what to do. Should he tell Gary about how Jesus healed him or just keep his mouth shut?

What would you do?

Divide the class into small discussion groups. Have the students discuss the following questions and then decide as a group how they would help Phil make his decision to share about Jesus or not.

♦ Phil said that God healed him. Why do you think that not everyone in the hospital was healed?

♦ Why did God tell Phil He was going to heal him?

♦ Do you believe that God sometimes uses medicine to heal people? Explain.

Relationship with God has its privileges.

Copies of Lesson 9 Secret Orders.

Even in the spy game, friends are important. Sometimes, though, it is tough to know who your friends are. One way to tell is by watching their actions. But remember, if you are watching them, they may also be watching you. Friendship has got to be a two-way street. Things can't always just be coming your way, you know.

So here is your assignment for this week. Draw a roadway with two lanes. At the beginning of the roadway, have a sign with your name on it. At the end of the roadway, have a sign marked for God. In each of the lanes have at least 5 cars. These cars will represent the benefits that come your way from a relationship with God and also the good things you are able to give back to God. Label each car with a benefit.

Remember to bring your completed Secret Orders to class next week.

Make sure the students in your class are confident about their salvation. Provide a time for students to seek the Lord and accept Christ as their Savior if they have not already done so.

SECRET ORDERS
Draw a roadway with two lanes. At the beginning of the roadway, have a sign with your name on it. At the end of the roadway, have a sign marked for God. In each of the lanes have at least five cars. These cars will represent the benefits that come your way from a relationship with God and also the good things you are able to give back to God.

GALATIANS MEMORY VERSES

Lesson 1	Galatians 1:9	I said this before. Now I say it again: You have already accepted the Good News. If anyone tells you another way to be saved, he should be condemned!
Lesson 2	Galatians 1:11-12	Brothers, I want you to know that the Good News I preached to you was not made by men. I did not get it from men, nor did any man teach it to me. Jesus Christ showed it to me.
Lesson 3	Galatians 6:10	When we have the opportunity to help anyone, we should do it. But we should give special attention to those who are in the family of believers.
Lesson 4	Galatians 6:2-3	Help each other with your troubles. When you do this, you truly obey the law of Christ. If anyone thinks that he is important when he is really not important, he is only fooling himself.
Lesson 5	Galatians 2:20	I do not live anymore—it is Christ living in me. I still live in my body, but I live by faith in the Son of God. He loved me and gave himself to save me.
Lesson 6	Galatians 4:4-5	But when the right time came, God sent his Son. His Son was born of a woman and lived under the law. God did this so that he could buy freedom for those who were under the law. His purpose was to make us his children.
Lesson 7	Galatians 2:21	This gift is from God, and it is very important to me. If the law could make us right with God, then Christ did not have to die.
Lesson 8	Galatians 5:13	My brothers, God called you to be free. But do not use your freedom as an excuse to do the things that please your sinful self. Serve each other with love.
Lesson 9	Galatians 5:16	So I tell you: Live by following the Spirit. Then you will not do what your sinful selves want.
Lesson 10	Galatians 5:25	We get our new life from the Spirit. So we should follow the Spirit.
Lesson 11	Galatians 5:17	Our sinful selves want what is against the Spirit. The Spirit wants what is against our sinful selves. The two are against each other. So you must not do just what you please.
Lesson 12	Galatians 5:22-23	But the Spirit gives love, joy, peace, patience, kindness, goodness, faithfulness, gentleness, self-control. There is no law that says these things are wrong.
Lesson 13	Galatians 6:9	We must not become tired of doing good. We will receive our harvest of eternal life at the right time. We must not give up!

ITEMS NEEDED FOR LESSON

challenge review

- ❑ Challenge notebooks
- ❑ Lesson 9 Secret Orders

more activities

1—Creative Writing

- ❑ *Club 56 Activity Zone* page 19
- ❑ Markers
- ❑ Assorted magazines
- ❑ Famous ads

opening activity

- ❑ *The Song of the King* by Max Lucado

2—Bible Study

- ❑ *Club 56 Activity Zone* page 20
- ❑ Pencils
- ❑ Bibles

bible lesson

- ❑ Dictionary
- ❑ Index cards
- ❑ Pencils
- ❑ Bibles
- ❑ Hamburger Helper
- ❑ Blanket
- ❑ Compass
- ❑ Megaphone (or drawing of megaphone)
- ❑ Puzzles (simple, children's)
- ❑ Blindfolds (two)
- ❑ Chalkboard
- ❑ Chalk

3—Game

- ❑ Styrofoam peanuts (large bag)
- ❑ Spoons (large, two)
- ❑ Paper bags (lunch-sized, two)

4—Music

- ❑ Posterboard
- ❑ Pen
- ❑ Songbooks
- ❑ Guitar (or piano)

memory verse activity

- ❑ Bibles
- ❑ Posterboard
- ❑ Construction paper
- ❑ Scissor
- ❑ Pencils
- ❑ Felt-tip pen
- ❑ Tape
- ❑ Tin cans (one per student, empty, clean)
- ❑ Can openers
- ❑ Milk cartons (small, empty)
- ❑ Nails
- ❑ Hammers
- ❑ Matches
- ❑ Candles (votive)
- ❑ Spray paint
- ❑ Newspaper
- ❑ Hair dryer

living it out

- ❑ None

challenge for the week

- ❑ Copies of Lesson 10 Secret Orders

SPECIAL NOTE

This week our Memory Verse states, "We get our new life from the Spirit. So we should follow the Spirit." Our mission statement tells us we are to "equip the body of Christ to bring children and youth into the kingdom and train them to walk and minister in the power of the Holy Spirit." I encourage you to effectively and prayerfully train your students.

The Holy Spirit: The ultimate companion.

We get our new life from the Spirit. So we should follow the Spirit.

Galatians 5:25

Luke 11:13; John 14:16,17; 16:7-15; Romans 1:4; 8:2; 1 Corinthians 3:16; 2 Corinthians 3:3; 13:14; Philippians 1:19; Hebrews 9:14;

A. So Who Is This Guy?

B. What Does This Guy Do?

C. What Do We Do?

EXPERIENCING THE FULLNESS OF THE SPIRIT

My husband and I walked into the hospital room on a rainy November night to meet our new bundle of joy. Our emotions welled up as we looked down at the most beautiful little face in the whole, entire world. Of course, that was a totally unbiased opinion. This tiny little boy was not flesh of our flesh, but the bond that formed at that instant could not have been any stronger.

Feelings are one thing, but as we later stood in front of the judge in a cold, impersonal courtroom, there was the realization of the legal commitment we would make to this child we loved. Our responsibility, as the judge explained it, was to care for our son as if he was our natural born child. The adoption then became final. The legal birth certificate issued by the state of Oregon had my name in the place marked for "mother." Seeing my name placed there gave me an incredible feeling.

When God looks down on us at the point of our new birth, He feels greater love than we can ever imagine. However, He goes beyond just loving us from afar. He legally adopts us as sons and daughters. He binds Himself to us legally. All that is His is also ours. God put His name on our heavenly birth certificate in the place marked for "father." Through His love, we become true children of the King.

Materials: Challenge notebooks and Lesson 9 Secret Orders.

How many of you drew a picture of a highway with the ten cars? Let's take time to see what benefits you listed on each car from having a relationship with God and what you can give back to Him.

Have the students place their completed Secret Orders in their Challenge notebooks.

Materials: *The Song of the King* by Max Lucado.

Note: This book is available from Word Publishing.

Even though you are all mature and totally cool kids, I hope you still like to hear a good story. I have an awesome one that I want to share with you today.

Allow the students to get into comfortable positions where they can listen to the story. Read this powerful story out loud to the class.

♦ How does this story remind us of our own walk?

Our lives are a lot like this story. As believers, we are on a journey through life. We live in a world of many struggles and temptations. Our goal is to serve Jesus and someday see Him in heaven. Our enemy Satan, though, is at work to distract and tempt us away from our goal. We are not in this fight alone. God has sent us the ultimate companion. This companion knows the King and will help us achieve our goals.

♦ Who is this ultimate companion?

Let's begin our lesson today and find out more about this friend that God has made available to us.

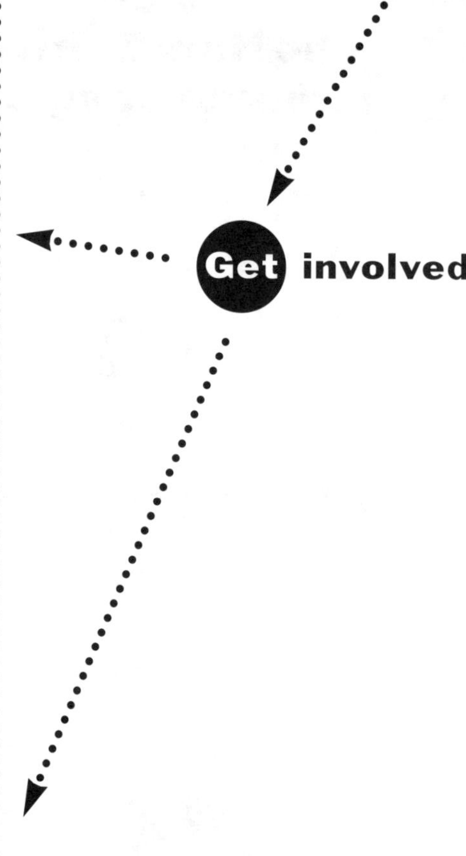

Read through the story several times before class. This will aid you in your fluency and expression.

The Holy Spirit: The ultimate companion.

During the activities, keep the groups small so that all have a chance to participate.

Materials: Dictionary, index cards, chalkboard, chalk, pencils, Bibles, Hamburger Helper, blanket, compass, megaphone (or drawing of megaphone),puzzles (simple, children's) and blindfolds (two).

Before class: Write the correct definitions for each of the following words on index cards: heir, guarantee, sealed, inheritance and redeemed.

In our Scripture today there are a number of words that we need to understand about our ultimate companion that God has given us. Let's play a game called Dictionary to see who knows the definitions of these important words.

(On the board write the following words: heir, guarantee, sealed, inheritance and redeemed. Divide the class into teams of two or three students. Give each team a pencil and five index cards.)

I have written the correct definition for each of the words on the board on my cards. Your job is to each write a plausible but phony definition. When you have thought up a definition, write one on each of the index cards. Sign your name to each of your cards.

(Collect the cards, adding yours to the others. Read the definitions in random order. After you have read all the definitions for one word, have each of the teams decide which one they think is correct. Each team scores five points for picking the correct definition. If any team chooses one of the incorrect definitions, the team whose member wrote it will be awarded three points. After the round, write the correct definition on the chalkboard by each word. Play until all five words have been used. When finished, add up the scores. The team with the highest score wins.)

♦ How do we become children of God?

♦ If we are a child, then we are an heir. What does it mean to be an heir of God?

♦ If we are a child of God, we are sealed with the Holy Spirit of promise. What does *sealed* mean?

♦ When we are sealed with the Holy Spirit of promise, what does He guarantee us?

When we believe and trust the Word of truth, which is the Good News of salvation through Jesus, God adopts us as sons and daughters. He gives us a gift, a companion to walk with us as long as we live.

So Who Is This Guy?

God has given us a companion with many names. These names help us to know all the ways our companion will help us. Luke 11:13 tells us the main name of our companion. Let's look up that verse to see what it says.

(Have the students look up the verse in their Bibles and identify the name of our companion.)

♦ **What is the name of our friend?**

The Holy Spirit is only one of the many names given to our companion. Let's see if we can find some other names.

(Have the students look up the following verses. Ask for volunteers to read each name out loud after they have found it.)

   1 Corinthians 3:16—*God's Spirit*

   John 14:17—*Spirit of truth, Helper*

   2 Corinthians 3:3—*Spirit of the living God*

   Romans 8:2—*Spirit that brings life*

   Philippians 1:19—*Spirit of Jesus Christ*

   Hebrews 9:14—*Eternal Spirit*

   Romans 1:4—*Spirit of holiness*

The Holy Spirit is one of the three parts of God. **Does that seem like a hard idea to wrap your brain around? Would it help you to understand it if I told you that I also have three parts to me?** *(Adapt to your own life.)* I am a mother, a daughter and a wife. In each of these roles I have a different job to do. *(Write these titles—mother, daughter and wife—on the board. Under each of the headings, have the students come up with some of the different duties or responsibilities for that person. Some will be the same, others will be specific to the particular person. In the same way, God is all one, but each part of God has a different job.)*

Let's find out what the specific jobs of God, the Holy Spirit and Jesus are. *(Have the students each look up 2 Cor. 13:14.)*

♦ **According to this verse, what is the function of Jesus? God? the Holy Spirit?**

Each part of God has a specific purpose. They all have a job that only they can do.

What Does This Guy Do?

So now we know that the Holy Spirit is God in the Spirit. He was sent to be our ultimate companion. But what exactly does He do and how does that help us?

In order to answer that question, I have brought along some items that might give you a clue. *(Lay out the blanket, Hamburger Helper, compass and megaphone.)* Each of these objects matches up with one of the jobs of the Holy Spirit. In order to figure out what those are, you will need to look up two Scripture references: John 14:16 and John 16:7–15. *(Have the students look up these Scripture verses.)*

Now let's see if you can match these objects to one of the words and tell how the object illustrates one of the four functions of the Holy Spirit. *(Ask for volunteers who would be willing to match up the items with the Scripture information. They should come up with the following: the blanket represents the comforter; the Hamburger Helper represents the Helper; the compass represents the guide in truth; the megaphone represents the witness for Jesus.)*

The Holy Spirit: The ultimate companion.

When you have a large number of Scripture verses to look up in a lesson, have the references written out on index cards. Give these to the students as they come into the classroom. They can look them up and mark the spot in their Bibles before class begins.

What Do We Do?

Does this ultimate companion sound like someone you would like to have on your side? Would you like to be His friend?

If you answered yes to the above questions, you might be wondering, *How do I make this guy my friend?* Well, the answer to that is simple. When we ask Jesus into our hearts, we get the help of this ultimate companion. It's like an extra bonus. All we need to do is seek the Holy Spirit and listen to His voice. He will let us know which way to go. He will help us put all of the pieces to the puzzles of our lives together. Let me demonstrate.

(Ask for three volunteers.) I am going to ask you to assemble a simple puzzle. You have one minute to put all of the pieces in the correct spots. *(Blindfold two of the volunteers. Have the third volunteer act as a helper to only one of the blindfolded participants. This helper is to whisper instructions into the ear of her friend. She can tell her everything she needs to help put the puzzle together.)* Ready? Go. *(Time the students for one minute.)*

♦ **Who was the most successful in putting the puzzle together?**

Life can be a lot like this little demonstration. We can try to get through it on our own, or we can tap into the help that the Holy Spirit wants to offer us. He can be our ultimate companion—the one Jesus left to give to us. Just like the knight in our opening story, who we choose to help us through life will determine if we are successful.

Conclusion

When Jesus left the earth, God the Father sent the Holy Spirit to be the ultimate companion for every believer in Jesus. The Holy Spirit is known by many names. Each name tells us something different about His role.

The Holy Spirit was sent by the Father to remind us of God's Word, to help us, to comfort us, to guide us in all righteousness and to point us to Jesus. We need to listen to the voice of the Holy Spirit to guide our lives. The Holy Spirit is our ultimate companion.

Galatians 5:25

We get our new life from the Spirit. So we should follow the Spirit.

Materials: Bibles, posterboard, construction paper, scissors, pencils, felt-tip pen, tape, tin cans (one per student. empty, clean), can openers, milk cartons (small, empty), nails, hammers, matches, candles (votive), spray paint, newspaper and hair dryer (if desired).

Note: If available, each student can be given her own votive candle to put inside her holder. If these are not available, one candle can be used to demonstrate and the students can use their own candles at home.

Our Memory Verse tells us that we should follow the Holy Spirit because we receive our new life from Him. One way we can follow Him is to follow in the footsteps of Jesus. Have construction paper, pencils and scissors available. Ask each student to trace her own footprint and cut it out. Then, the student can find the Memory Verse in the Bible and write it on the footprint. When the students are finished, they can tape their footprints to the classroom wall.

As we learned today, the Holy Spirit has many different titles because of the many characteristics He brings to our lives. Often, the Holy Spirit is represented by a flame.

♦ Why is a flame used to represent Him?

♦ What other words represent the Holy Spirit?

Brainstorm with the class words they think of that describe the Holy Spirit or things that represent Him. Write the responses on the posterboard.

Now we are going to make candleholders. The flame inside and the design of the holder will help us to remember the many wonderful characteristics that the Holy Spirit offers us.

To make the candleholders, complete the following steps:

1. Give each student a can, a small milk carton, a nail and a pencil. Have can openers and hammers for the students to share.

2. Instruct the students to take the remaining lid off each can with a can opener. Watch out for sharp edges.

3. Each student should decide on a design or words that represent the Holy Spirit and lightly sketch it onto the can. Then put the milk carton inside of the can to help it hold its shape.

4. Sharing the hammers, the students should use a nail to hammer small holes in the cans according to the patterns they have traced onto their cans. The holes do not need to touch, but should be close enough that the design or words can be understood.

5. If desired, the students can place the cans on newspapers outside and spray them with any chosen color of spray paint. The students can take turns drying their cans with a hair dryer.

6. If each student has her own votive candle, she can carefully light it and place her candle holder around it to see the light shine through her design. If students do not have individual candles, they can take turns putting their cans around the class candle. They can use their own candles at home.

The Holy Spirit: The ultimate companion.

1—Creative Writing

Materials: *Club 56 Activity Zone* page 19, markers, assorted magazines and famous ads.

The Holy Spirit is our ultimate friend and companion. He does so many cool things in our lives: He gives us gifts, empowers us, comforts us and guides us. These are just a few of the things He does.

All of you here at Club 56 have the opportunity to hear about the good things the Holy Spirit does. But what about those who aren't in our class? How will they come to know this ultimate companion?

Good news! You have just been hired by a prestigious Manhattan advertising agency. Your assignment is to come up with a catchy slogan to let others know about the Holy Spirit and what He does.

Take some time to review with the students examples of famous ads from different companies, such as Nike ("Just do it!"), Allstate ("You're in Good Hands"), Kentucky Fried Chicken ("Finger Lickin' Good"), National Dairy Council (MILK – "Where's Your Mustache?") and Timex ("Takes a Licking and Keeps On Ticking"). Talk about the images that go with the slogan and how they are all designed to grab attention as well as convey information.

Hand out the activity pages. Allow the students some time to work on their slogans. When the students are done, have them share their ads.

2—Bible Study

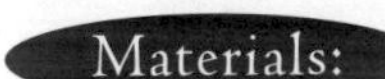
Materials: *Club 56 Activity Zone* page 20, pencils and Bibles.

The Bible gives us many examples of times when the Holy Spirit was the ultimate companion and helper to God's people. Some of these stories you may be familiar with, and others may be new to you. Try to discover, as you read through the Scripture, not only who the Holy Spirit helped but how He helped them.

3—Game

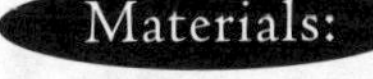
Materials: Styrofoam peanuts (large bag), spoons (large, two) and paper bags (lunch-sized, two).

The focus of our lesson today is experiencing the fullness of the Holy Spirit. We want to learn to walk closely and be guided by God's Spirit. In order to do that, we need to turn away from our natural or fleshly feelings. Instead of doing only what we feel like doing, we want to pursue what God has for us.

We are going to play a short game to help us remember that we want to walk in the fullness of the Spirit. To play this game, I am going to assign you to teams and ask you to fill something—not just partially—but to the fullest.

Activity Zone page 19

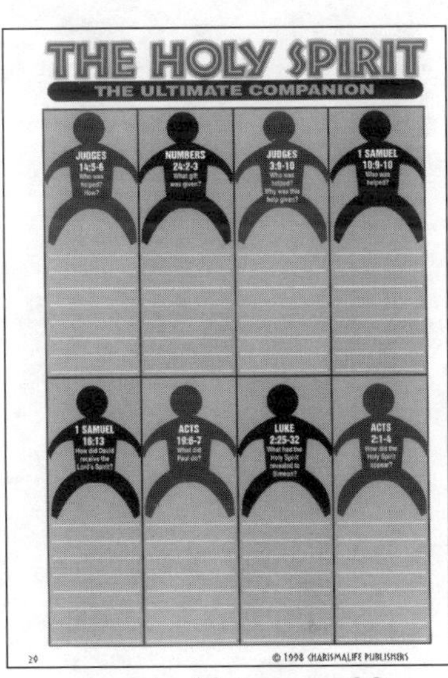

Activity Zone page 20

Divide the class into equal teams. Have them line up at one end of the room in a relay fashion. At the other end of the room, place the lunch bags. On the go signal, the first team member will scoop up Styrofoam peanuts from the large bag with the spoon and proceed as quickly as possible to the lunch bag where she will deposit the peanuts. Any peanuts that fall from the spoon or don't make it into the bag are considered dead. After dumping the peanuts into the lunch bag, she runs back and tags the next team member. This continues until one of the teams fills their lunch bag.

4—Music

Materials: Posterboard, pen, songbooks and guitar (or piano).

Our Power Point tells us that the Holy Spirit is our ultimate companion. There are over 50 different names the Bible has for the Holy Spirit because of His many wonderful characteristics. Let's see how many titles we can remember! Ask students to call out different titles of the Holy Spirit as you write them on the posterboard.

As we can see from the things we wrote down, the Holy Spirit has many characteristics that He brings to our lives. We are going to take a few of these and come up with some songs we can sing together in worship.

Divide the class into four groups. Give the students songbooks and encourage each of the groups to come up with a familiar song that relates to one of the following characteristics of the Holy Spirit:

Group 1: comforter

Group 2: holiness

Group 3: Spirit of God

Group 4: eternal life

After the students have come up with the songs for worship, begin the worship time with prayer. Then lead the group in singing the four chosen songs. If desired, a guitar can accompany the singing.

The Holy Spirit: The ultimate companion.

"I hate starting a new school! Why do we always have to move?"

Lisa's mom smiled. "Honey, I know this isn't easy, but the Forest Service needs Dad's help. His specialty in watershed management is critical to this area's economy."

Lisa rolled her eyes dramatically. "Mom, I don't even know what that means. All I know is that I just make a friend and I have to move again. To you and Dad it's an adventure, but to me, it's more time alone in my room." She tried to sound casual, but her mother knew how hard it really was for Lisa.

"I'll tell you what, let's pray for your day, OK?" Lisa nodded wordlessly. "Lord Jesus," prayed her mom, "I pray that your precious Holy Spirit will go with Lisa today and be her companion and guide. Help her to remember to call on you whenever she feels sad or alone. And please give her Christian friends or kids whom she can lead to You. In Your name, amen. Lisa, would you like to pray?" Lisa told her mom that she didn't want to this time. "OK," said her mom, "then off you go. You're not going alone, Lisa, remember that. Jesus is always with you. I'll see you after school."

The morning went well for Lisa. Although most of the kids ignored her, she was able to find her classes. It was a relief to find that she was ahead in most subjects.

Finding the cafeteria was the hardest part of the day. After Lisa got her lunch tray, she walked around looking for a place to sit. When she finally found a place to sit, she started to put her tray down. "Hey," shouted one of the girls who was sitting there, "that place is taken. Sit somewhere else." As she walked away, Lisa heard them laughing. She tossed her tray on a nearby table and walked out of the cafeteria.

Lisa stood looking up the hallway. She was desperate. She had never felt so alone in her life. What could she do? What would you do?

Can you help Lisa?

Divide the class into small discussion groups. Have each group discuss the questions below and be prepared to share their answers with the entire class.

- What did Lisa's mom pray before Lisa left for school?
- How does the Holy Spirit help us when we are afraid?
- Would you really take time to pray if you felt alone or afraid?

Materials: Copies of Lesson 10 Secret Orders.

We have been on the trail of one of the most difficult-to-follow secret agents ever. I mean, talk about your man of mystery. Wow, this Holy Spirit fellow is one undercover guy. In spite of our best effort to put a tail on Him, He always seems to be just a bit ahead of us. He always gives us the slip.

Your job this week is to find out three things about the Holy Spirit that you don't already know. Your don't have to reveal your sources. You can get your information from the Bible or through clandestine interviews. It's up to you.

Be sure to report back in a week with the information you have uncovered.

Remember to bring your completed Secret Orders to class next week.

SECRET ORDERS
Find out three things about the Holy Spirit that you don't already know. Be sure to report back next week with the information you have uncovered.

GALATIANS POWER POINTS

Lesson 1	:	Discover God by knowing Jesus.
Lesson 2	:	God's truth is nothing but the truth.
Lesson 3	:	The team concept: Created by God.
Lesson 4	:	It's what we have in common that counts.
Lesson 5	:	Faith is taking God at His Word.
Lesson 6	:	Calling all people: God's family is for you.
Lesson 7	:	The law: A foundation for freedom.
Lesson 8	:	God can make a way.
Lesson 9	:	Relationship with God has its privileges.
Lesson 10	:	The Holy Spirit: The ultimate companion.
Lesson 11	:	The Spirit-filled life: A walk on the right side.
Lesson 12	:	Fruits and gifts: The gifts that keep on giving.
Lesson 13	:	Forever freedom comes from following the Father.

ITEMS NEEDED FOR LESSON

❏ Challenge notebooks
❏ Lesson 10 Secret Orders
❏ Chalkboard
❏ Chalk

❏ Healthy plant (or tree or drawing of tree)
❏ Construction paper
❏ Scissors
❏ Hole punch
❏ String
❏ Markers
❏ Bibles

❏ Bibles
❏ Plant (from Opening Activity)
❏ Dead tree (or picture of dead tree)
❏ Index cards

❏ Index cards
❏ Bibles
❏ Watch with second hand
❏ Pen

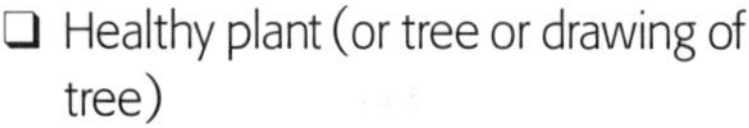

❏ Copies of Living It Out story

1—Individual Art

❏ *Club 56 Activity Zone* page 21
❏ Shoelaces (white, one pair for each student)
❏ Pencils
❏ Markers (fine-tipped, colored)

2—Object Lesson

❏ Index cards
❏ Pencils

3—Drama

❏ Slips of paper (nine)
❏ Bowl
❏ Pen

4—Problem Solving

❏ *Club 56 Activity Zone* page 22
❏ Pencils

❏ Copies of Lesson 11 Secret Orders

SPECIAL NOTE

You will need two plants for this week's lesson. If at all possible, bring one in with a healthy growth of leaves and another one that is dead. When we teach with object lessons that clarify the truth, 5th and 6th graders will understand those truths much more clearly

The Spirit-filled life: A walk on the right side.

Our sinful selves want what is against the Spirit. The Spirit wants what is against our sinful selves. The two are against each other. So you must not do just what you please.

Galatians 5:17

Galatians 5:16-22

A. The Battle Lines Are Drawn

B. Whose Side Are You On?

C. Alive and Well and Bearing Fruit

WHAT IS THE SPIRIT-FILLED LIFE?

I grew up in the fruitful Willamette Valley of Oregon. From spring to fall there was fresh fruit everywhere. In the summer after a day of picking strawberries, I would head for the public swimming pool. Our pool was old, outdoors and unheated. The water never got very warm, and I would have to keep fairly active to remain in it for long. When I was through swimming, I would be hungry once again. Fortunately, on the bike ride home there were always apples hanging over the fences begging to be picked and eaten.

One of my best summer memories is sitting on top of the grape arbor in the Whitlow's vacant lot with the rest of the neighborhood gang. The big Concord grapes hung thick in juicy purple clusters. I remember asking myself, *How could this happen?* No one cared for the arbor. All of the grapes were ones that grew naturally; growing in good soil, abundant rain and just enough sunshine to ripen them.

Our spiritual fruit will come just like the grapes on the Whitlow's arbor. We can't make the fruit grow, but we can help by planting ourselves in the good soil of the Word of God, keeping open to the filling of the Holy Spirit and grafting ourselves into God's perfect Son. As we plug into these three things, the character of Jesus will show up in our lives. The fruit of our lives should be as evident as the big clusters of grapes hanging from the Whitlow's arbor. The fruit of the Holy Spirit is what puts our faith into everyday actions. Without them we will never produce a harvest. Here's to a fruit-filled week!

Materials: Challenge notebooks, Lesson 10 Secret Orders, chalkboard and chalk.

Have your students share with the rest of the class the three new things they learned about the Holy Spirit. Write their answers on the chalkboard. Then have a time of prayer, asking the Holy Spirit to make Himself known to you and to your class this week in several of the ways that are on the chalkboard.

Have the students place their completed Secret Orders in their Challenge notebooks.

Materials: Healthy plant (or tree or drawing of tree), construction paper, scissors, hole punch, string, markers and Bibles.

Before class: Bring a large healthy plant into your classroom. The plant needs to be able to support nine, 3-inch paper fruits from its branches. Make fruit shapes (about 3 inches in diameter) out of construction paper. Write one fruit of the Spirit (love, joy, peace, patience, kindness, goodness, faithfulness, gentleness and self-control) on each shape. Prepare extra blank shapes for the children to use in the activity.

Today in our lesson we are going to look at what the Spirit-filled life looks like. Divide the class into small groups. Pass out the fruits equally among each of the groups. **When we talk about the Spirit, we usually think about the good things He brings into our lives. We call these good things** *fruit.* **So being the exceptionally clever teacher that I am, I have cut out some fruit shapes to help us remember these good things.**

I would like you to think of different ways that kids your age could act out the word on the fruit your group has been given. Write those actions on the extra blank fruit. For example, for the word kindness, you might write: kindness is sitting with a new kid at lunch. Take five minutes and try to think of as many active ways as you can to describe your fruit. We are going to use these fruits later in the lesson.

When the time is up and the students have completed their fruits, have them hang them from the plant using the string and hole punch.

It is a good thing to know about the fruit of the Spirit. It is an even better thing to put those gifts into action. Our lives are meant to reflect the things we believe.

The Spirit-filled life: A walk on the right side.

Your 5th and 6th grade students are being encouraged to make their faith their own. Part of helping them with this transition is getting them to think about how they can apply their faith to everyday life.

Materials: Bibles, plant (from Opening Activity), dead tree (or picture of dead tree) and index cards.

Note: The dead tree can be made with a pot of dry soil with a dead branch stuck in it.

The Battle Lines Are Drawn

Did you know there has been a major war going on that has lasted for thousands of years? This battle that has been going on since sin entered the world is the fight between our flesh (sometimes called our evil nature) and what the Holy Spirit wants us to do. Even as believers in Jesus we have a battle that goes on between our flesh and our spiritual nature. Our flesh wants to "do its own thing." Doing our own thing is called *sin*. Instead, we need to do what God wants us to do. That is not always easy. But remember, God has given us a companion, a Helper to help us walk through life on the right side. Let's open our Bibles and find out some more about this battle that is going on in each of us. *(Have the students turn in their Bibles to Gal. 5:16-17. Ask for a volunteer to read the verses out loud.)*

♦ **What does this mean?**

To help show you what this means, let's have an arm wrestling contest. **Who would like to enter?** The contest is open to anyone who would like to meet this challenge. *(You may arm wrestle against the students or you may bring in another adult helper to participate. Once you have a couple of volunteers, have someone tell them secretly that if at any time during the match they need help, all they have to do is ask and it will be given to them. When one asks for help, either you [if you are not arm wrestling] or a helper can put your hand on top of the student's hand and give him an extra amount of push.)*

In this match, you were struggling against someone. In life, we are fighting against our flesh. However, just as you were allowed to call for help and receive it, you can also do the same thing in life.

Verse 16 says that we are to "live by following the Spirit."

♦ **What does that mean? How do you get help from an invisible companion?**

Whose Side Are You On?

(Bring out the healthy plant that the students decorated with the paper fruits. Also bring out the dead tree.) In this battle we are engaged in, we have a choice as to which side we are on. One side represents life and the other brings death. These trees here are representative of the two choices we have. We can choose to walk on the right side by listening to and obeying the Holy Spirit. That will give us a healthy, fruitful life. Or we can choose to walk on the wrong side by listening to our flesh. That will bring us a dead, unproductive life.

Let's take a look at the dead tree first.

♦ **What caused this tree to be so unhealthy?** *(Allow time for the students to come up with some reasons.)*

You have come up with some really good reasons for why this tree died. This tree has bad soil, it hasn't been watered and it hasn't been fertilized.

♦ **Do you think this tree could produce fruit?** *(Allow for responses.)*

This tree is like us when we don't walk with the Spirit. Even if we believe in Jesus, if we don't read our Bibles or listen to the Spirit daily, the flesh can win the struggle. A life without the Holy Spirit's help will only produce bad fruit.

Turn with me to Galatians 5:19-21 and take a look to see if we can find out what those bad fruits might be. *(Ask for a volunteer to read these verses out loud for the rest of the class.)*

♦ **What are some of the bad fruits?**

♦ **Do you see anything in the list that happens in your life?**

♦ **What is something you can do to eliminate this from your life?**

Alive and Well and Bearing Fruit

None of us wants to be like the dead tree, right? We all would like to have fruit-filled lives. So how do we do that? Let's look again at the healthy plant.

♦ **What are some of things that are right with this plant?** *The soil is good; it looks like it gets plenty of water.*

Do you think that a healthy plant has to work to grow fruit? Now this may be a surprise, but plants that are properly cared for automatically bear fruit. Believe it or not, that is just like us. If we plant ourselves in the good soil of God's Word and water ourselves by being filled with the Holy Spirit, then the fruit of the Spirit will automatically be a part of our lives.

Let's look at Galatians 5:22-23. *(Ask someone to read it out loud to the rest of the class.)* In the Opening Activity you wrote what the fruit would look like when seen in your life. Let's look at those actions to see what walking in the Spirit looks like. *(Review the fruits that are hanging on the good plant and allow the students to explain the actions they thought up for each fruit.)*

Remember, walking with the Spirit is not just some wonderful spiritual experience. It is an everyday thing. It is putting what we believe into action.

Conclusion

If someone asked us to choose between life and death, the answer would be simple. All of us would choose life. However, each day we make decisions that will feed our fleshly nature or our spiritual man. If we feed the flesh, it will lead us to spiritual death. However, if we feed the spiritual man it will bring us new strength for life. The Bible tells us to "follow in the Spirit." Each day we need to listen for His voice and do what He is asking us to do. The Holy Spirit is the person God has given us to fight the battle against our flesh. His gifts help us to bear fruit and win this battle. He is our ultimate friend and companion.

Remind the kids that we all struggle. However, if we confess our sins, God is always faithful to forgive us (1 John 1:9). Also remind the kids that at times, we all need additional help.

Galatians 5:17

Our sinful selves want what is against the Spirit. The Spirit wants what is against our sinful selves. The two are against each other. So you must not do just what you please.

Activity Zone page 21

Materials: Index cards, Bibles, watch with second hand and pen.

Before class: Write the Memory Verse on the cards, one word per card.

We have a long Memory Verse today—one that might challenge your memory banks. Let's work together as a class to try to memorize it perfectly.

Allow the students several minutes to study the verse. They can practice with each other to review the verse. Show them that the first two sentences are opposites. Mix up the verse cards you wrote before class and hand them out to the students until they are all gone.

Hopefully you have all committed the verse to memory. We are going to work as a class and try to correctly assemble the Memory Verse. When it is time for your word, you will need to run up here to the board and stand in place. Watch for when your word is needed because I am going to time you to see how fast we can do it.

Begin the game and time the students. You may want to repeat the game and give the class a chance to beat their time.

1—Individual Art

Materials: *Club 56 Activity Zone* page 21, shoelaces (white, one pair for each student), pencils and markers (fine-tipped, colored).

When we allow the Spirit to guide us, we walk on the right side of life. If we allow our flesh to control us, then we will find ourselves walking in places we shouldn't go.

To help remind us to walk with the Spirit, we are going to decorate a pair of shoelaces to put into our shoes. As we walk along, they will be good reminders of the right way to walk.

Give each student a pair of shoelaces. Have the students use the worksheet to experiment with different designs they might want to put on their laces. Suggestions might be Christian symbols, words that tell the gifts of the Spirit or simple designs. Once the students are satisfied with the model on the worksheet, have them begin to work on their shoelaces.

2—Object Lesson

Materials: Index cards and pencils.

How many of you like to be right? It's kind of embarrassing to give a wrong answer or impart a piece of wrong information, isn't it? Well, I am going to teach you a trick today—one that you will always be able to answer correctly.

Hand out three index cards to each student. On one card have them write the number 1 on the front and the number 2 on the back. On the second card, have the students write the number 3 on the front and the number 4 on the back. On the last card, have the students write the number 5 on the front and the number 6 on the back.

Once the cards are numbered, have the students lay the cards out in front of them so that the numbers 2, 4 and 6 are face up. Tell the students to pick **one** of the cards and turn it over so that the number on the other side is showing (this number will be a 1, 3 or 5).

I will now guess the sum total of all the numbers that you have facing up. Choose one student and without looking at his numbers, tell him that his numbers total 11. Am I right? Are you amazed? Let me demonstrate for you once again. Choose a second student. Have this student look at the first student's numbers to make sure that his are different. Now tell this student that his total is also 11.

♦ Didn't I tell you I was always right?

♦ Have you figured out how I am able to be right each time?

In this object lesson I was able to always get the right answer because of a math trick. In real life, if we want to have the right answers, we need to walk with the Spirit.

Always practice the object lesson at least once before doing it before the class. This will ensure that the lesson will go smoothly and the point will be made.

3—Drama

Materials: Slips of paper (nine), bowl and pen.

Before class: On each of nine small slips of paper, write one of the following words: love, joy, peace, patience, kindness, goodness, faithfulness, gentleness and self-control. Fold the slips in half and put them into a bowl.

When we hang around people enough, some of their habits rub off on us.

♦ Have you ever been told that you and your friends talk alike? act alike? In what ways are you and your friends alike?

♦ Do you have some of the same habits as other people in your family? What behaviors or attitudes do you have in common?

♦ Have you heard people say that some owners look like their dogs? Do you think this is true? How could this happen?

♦ Why do you think we start to act and talk like our family members or friends? *Because we spend so much time together.*

When we spend time with others, we are bound to pick up some of their characteristics. The same thing happens when we walk with the Holy Spirit. The characteristics of God can start to be seen in our lives. Today we talked about the fruit of the Spirit. Now we are going to play a game of charades and see if we can remember all the fruits that can be seen in our lives if we live Spirit–filled lives.

Divide the class into two teams. Have one member from each team come to the front of the room. Ask one student to draw a slip of paper from the bowl. The two students will read the word and simultaneously act out the fruit of the Spirit that is written on the slip. The students must only use actions, without talking, to describe the word. The first team to guess the word receives a point. Then two more volunteers will draw a slip of paper and perform the charade. The team with the most points after the nine charades is the winner.

4—Problem Solving

Materials: *Club 56 Activity Zone* page 22 and pencils.

In our lesson, we talked about what a Spirit-filled life looks like. If we stay close to the Lord, the fruit of the Spirit will be seen in our lives. We are going to do a puzzle in which you will have to solve some problems. You will read a description and then must come up with the fruit of the Spirit that is being described. Read the directions carefully at the top of the page before beginning.

Give the students time to complete the puzzle. Help the students with the directions if needed.

Activity Zone page 22

ANSWERS:
1. Faithfulness
2. Gentleness
3. Self-control
4. Patience
5. Peace
6. Love
7. Kindness
8. Goodness
9. Joy

SOLUTION:
The fruits of the Spirit are evidence of the Holy Spirit in my life.

Materials: Copies of Living It Out story.

Hi, I'm John V. Emerson, Jr. I don't know if it will do me any good, but I need to talk to someone. I know that this will sound really bad to you, but I can't stand my stepdad. I suppose you think I'm a pretty worthless person, don't you?

It's just that every time I'm in the house he is yelling at me. I can't seem to do anything right. To make matters worse, I'm a Christian and he's not. Every time I say anything back to him my mom looks at me like I'm the one who ought to know better. It's just not fair. I have a right to not like him. He expects me to do chores the minute I get home from school. He can't stand it if the family room gets messy at all, and he even inspects my room after I clean it. The guy makes a drill sergeant look lazy!

My mom loves to tell me that I should be loving and kind to him. Well, when he shows me a little slack I'll think about being all loving and kind.

Yesterday he found out that I left his dumb lawnmower out overnight. He grounded me for a week! I told him that he isn't my real dad and didn't have the right to tell me anything. He got so mad that he took off in his car. I wish I had just said OK, because now my mom is praying and crying her eyes out.

You know what? I think she blames me for the whole thing. She told me that I'm letting my temper rule my life. She said that I should be asking the Holy Spirit for help. To be honest, I don't really know how that works. Do you?

So, here I am in the middle of this big crisis and I really could use God's help. I guess I really do need to change. Do I just pray? Have you ever faced anything like this before?

Will you talk it over and get back to me? Good! I really need help.

Can you help John?

Divide the class into small discussion groups. Give each group a copy of the Living It Out story and the questions listed below. Tell the small groups to be prepared to share how they would help John after their discussion.

♦ Why is John so upset with his stepfather?

♦ How did John treat his stepfather?

♦ What works of the flesh do you see at work in John?

♦ How does the Holy Spirit help someone as angry as John?

Materials: Copies of Lesson 11 Secret Orders.

Our organization is looking for a new badge or emblem that all of us spies will wear to identify us. The Big Boss is looking for something that will identify us as being on the side of righteousness. We're the good guys, don't you know.

Come up with a sketch or a design on your worksheet. You could even create a real badge if you are so inclined.

Think about what being the good guys is all about—what we represent and how important it is to stand up for the right things. Work hard. We all want to see what kind of badge you are able to create.

Remember to bring your completed Secret Orders to class next week.

SECRET ORDERS
Design a new badge or emblem that will represent our organization. It needs to reflect who we are and what we believe.

ITEMS NEEDED FOR LESSON

❏ Lesson 11 Secret Orders
❏ Tape

1—Creative Writing

❏ *Club 56 Activity Zone* page 24
❏ Pens

2—Cooking

❏ *Club 56 Activity Zone* page 23
❏ Bibles
❏ Pencils
❏ Kabob sticks (wooden)
❏ Bowls (small)
❏ Fruits (assorted)
❏ Knife
❏ Napkins

❏ Index cards
❏ Play dough (three colors)
❏ Pen

❏ Lamp (small)
❏ Toy car (battery-operated)
❏ Boxes (nine, small)
❏ Wrapping paper
❏ Index cards (12)
❏ Pen

3—Group Art

❏ Construction paper (colored)
❏ Scissors
❏ Markers
❏ Paper bag (small)
❏ Tape (double-stick)
❏ Watch with second hand

❏ Bibles
❏ Paper
❏ Pencils

4—Outreach Project

❏ Fruit trees (several, small)
❏ Potting soil
❏ Shovel (small)
❏ Watering can

❏ Copies of Living It Out story

❏ Copies of Lesson 12 Secret Orders

SPECIAL NOTE

This week's lesson deals with the fruit and gifts of the Holy Spirit. As you prepare for your lesson, I encourage you to read the following Scripture: Romans 12; 1 Corinthians 12; Galatians 5; Ephesians 4:1-16 and Hebrews 2:1-4. If time permits, you may want to list the gifts for your students to discuss.

Fruits and gifts: The gifts that keep on giving.

But the Spirit gives love, joy, peace, patience, kindness, goodness, faithfulness, gentleness, self-control. There is no law that says these things are wrong.

Galatians 5:22-23

Luke 24:49; John 1:33; Acts 1: 5,8; 19:2; 1 Corinthians 12:7-11; Galatians 5:21-25; Ephesians 5:18

A. The Spirit at Work

B. Trains, Planes and Toy Cars

C. The Gifts That Keep on Giving

SO, WHAT'S THE DIFFERENCE BETWEEN FRUITS AND GIFTS?

It was a special morning at church. It was teacher appreciation Sunday, and I waited excitedly in the church foyer to hand out the appreciation gifts I had so lovingly picked out and wrapped. As the children's pastor at our church, it was my responsibility to thank our faithful teachers.

I love to give gifts, but my enthusiasm was dampened briefly that day as I gave a gift to one of my teachers. She didn't want it. It seems that she already had the book I was giving, and she didn't want another copy.

It didn't matter what her reason was for not wanting the gift. My feelings were hurt. Didn't she realize how much time I had spent to find just the right gift for her? How could she "blow off" my gesture with so little consideration?

That morning I got a small glimpse of how God must feel when we "blow off" the gifts that He offers to us, gifts which He has lovingly prepared.

Though I am sure none of us would intentionally snub a gift from God, that is what we do when we limit the work He desires to accomplish in our lives. Things we accept as simply our own shortcomings ("I've always had a quick temper" or "It's impossible for me to forgive them for what they did to me") are like turning our backs on the gifts that are ours for the taking.

Are there any of God's good gifts which you have refused or set aside? Take time this week to pray about that and to search your heart. Remember, nothing is impossible with God. Take hold of the gift that is just for you. Unwrap it. It is probably what you have been looking for.

Materials: Lesson 11 Secret Orders and tape.

How many of you created an emblem for our organization? Why don't a few of you share your creations, and then we will put all of them up on the wall for a few weeks.

Materials: Index cards, play dough (three colors) and pen.

Before class: Make three sets of cards with the following words written, one per card: lamp, car and gifts.

Have any of you ever played the game Pictionary? If students are unfamiliar with the game, explain to them how to play it. (The object of this game is to get team members to say the word you have been given by drawing a picture of it.)

Divide the class into three teams. Have each team pick one member who will be their sculptor.

The object of our game is to guess what the word on the card is before the other teams. Each team has a sculptor. The sculptor will look at the word on the card and use only play dough (no words) to give clues to help his team guess the correct word. For example, if your word were *Jesus,* you might make a cross. Understand?

Repeat the game for each word. Change the sculptor with each new word.

Believe it or not, these three words are the keys to our lesson on how the Holy Spirit works. Let's begin our lesson to find out what a lamp, a car and gifts have to do with the Holy Spirit.

Get involved

Fruits and gifts: The gifts that keep on giving.

GIFTS:

1. Wisdom
2. Knowledge
3. Faith
4. Healing
5. Miracles
6. Prophecy
7. Discernment
8. Tongues
9. Interpretation

Materials: Lamp (small), toy car (battery-operated), boxes (nine, small), wrapping paper, index cards (12) and pen.

Before class: Write one gift of the Spirit (1 Cor. 12:8-10) on each of nine index cards. Put a card in each box. Gift wrap the small boxes. Write the word *power* on one index card, *fruit* on another and *gifts* on a third. Set the objects out on a table in the following order: the lamp, the car and the wrapped gift boxes. Place the table near an outlet so the lamp can be plugged in during the lesson.

The Spirit at Work

In our lesson today we are going to look at three ways the Holy Spirit wants to work in our lives. I have placed three items on the table to help us remember how the Holy Spirit can work. *(Show the class each one of the objects on the table.)* We have a lamp, a battery-operated toy car and a group of gifts. One of these represents power, one represents fruit and one represents gifts. Let's start with the hard one.

♦ **Which one of these three items represents fruit?** *(Allow for answers and for students to give their reasons. If they have too much difficulty, begin with the obvious representation: gifts. Finally, place the gift sign in front of the boxes of gifts, the fruit sign in front of the lamp, and the power sign by the toy car.)*

♦ **Were you surprised that we placed the fruit sign in front of the lamp?** *(Allow the students to try to make a connection between the lamp and how it represents fruit.)*

The lamp represents each one of us. When we just sit there, we don't work. So what do we need to do? We need to get plugged in! The electricity represents the Holy Spirit.

♦ **When we plug in the lamp, what happens?** *The light comes on.*

The light represents Jesus. The fruit of the Spirit is the character of Jesus. Just as the light flows through the lamp, so will the character traits of Jesus when we are plugged into the Holy Spirit.

♦ **Who can remember all nine fruits of the Spirit?**

To plug into the Spirit, we need to walk in the Spirit.

♦ **How do we do that?** *(Allow for student responses.)*

We need to plug into the Holy Spirit and let Him fill us up. Then we will be a light to shine for all to see. The actions that will shine out of us are love, joy, peace, patience, kindness, goodness, faithfulness and self-control.

Trains, Planes and Toy Cars

(Place the toy car on the floor and allow it to run around for a minute.)

♦ **How does this toy car help us to remember the power of the Holy Spirit?** *The car represents us.*

♦ **What do the batteries represent?** *The batteries symbolize the Holy Spirit.*

He is the one that gives us the power. Let's look up some Scripture verses that will help us to understand more about the Holy Spirit. *(Assign the following verses to specific students to look up and then read out loud.)*

John 1:33	Luke 24:49	Acts 1:5
Acts 1:8	Acts 19:2	Ephesians 5:18

The Holy Spirit works in every believer. When we ask Jesus to be our Savior, the Holy Spirit comes to live in us and becomes our companion. However, every believer needs to answer the question of Acts 19:2. *(Have a student reread this verse.)*

♦ **Have any of you received the Holy Spirit since you believed?**

There is a separate filling of the Holy Spirit which is also called the baptism in the Holy Spirit.

♦ **How do we know that we are to receive the Holy Spirit?** *Jesus promised it to all of His followers. (See Luke 24:49 and Acts 1:5.)*

♦ **What happens to the followers who receive the Holy Spirit?** *The power of the Holy Spirit is given to them. (See Acts 1:8.)*

When Jesus' followers received the empowering of the Holy Spirit, they were able to do amazing things. The book of Acts records some of things they were able to do. They boldly preached the message of Christ, performed miracles and healings and even spoke in unknown languages.

Let's get back to the car. **Will the car look the same if we take out the batteries? Will the car run without batteries? If you put batteries in the car, will it run forever?**

The car will only go as long as the batteries give it power. Even though it will continue to look the same, the car will be dead and useless. This is like our spiritual life. We need to be constantly filling up our lives with the power of the Holy Spirit.

The Gifts That Keep on Giving

Our last objects up here are these boxes of gifts. **How many of you like to receive gifts?** Turn with me to 1 Corinthians 12:7-11. *(Read these verses to the class.)*

♦ **According to verse 11, who gives these gifts?**

♦ **Looking at verse 7, to whom does the Spirit give the gifts?**

♦ **Again in verse 7, for what are the gifts given?**

Let's take a look at our packages and see what is inside each of them. *(Choose nine students to open up the packages one at a time. When the student opens the gift, have him read the enclosed card that tells one of the gifts of the Holy Spirit.)*

Encourage all of the students to look up the Scripture references that are given even if they are not going to be reading it out loud. This will help them to become familiar with their Bibles.

Now would be a good time to ask if anyone would like to be baptized in the Holy Spirit. CharismaLife's "New Kid in the Spirit" is a pamphlet that gives step-by-step instructions on leading someone in the baptism in the Holy Spirit.

Fruits and gifts: The gifts that keep on giving.

♦ Do you recognize any of the gifts of the Holy Spirit in your life?

♦ How do you use this gift?

♦ Can you possess all of the gifts of the Holy Spirit? *All of the fruits of the Spirit are available to us, but from the wording it would seem that certain gifts are given according to what God's purpose is for you.*

Conclusion

God wants all of us to be empowered by His Holy Spirit. The Holy Spirit is a gift that God gives to us. He has specific fruit and gifts that He wants to add to our lives. These enable us to live the way God has asked us to live.

God's Spirit is available to all of us, and so are the good things that He brings. He wants to give us the gifts that keep on giving.

Galatians 5:22-23

But the Spirit gives love, joy, peace, patience, kindness, goodness, faithfulness, gentleness, self-control. There is no law that says these things are wrong.

Materials: Bibles, paper and pencils.

Use the following Scripture references: Matthew 3:10, Matthew 7:16-20, Luke 13:6, John 15:2 and John 15:16.

In each of the verses that I am going to assign, a symbol is being used to illustrate an important point. In each group I want you to discover what the symbol is, what point Jesus was trying to make and why He used the symbol that He did. I also want you to figure out if that symbol would be appropriate for us today. If you think that it might need to be changed, come up with a symbol that 5th and 6th graders might be able to understand more clearly. Be prepared to share what you have learned when we regroup.

Divide the students into five groups. Assign each group a Scripture. Write the questions they are to resolve on the board.

Each of the verses the students are looking up uses the symbol of fruit. **The message is to be fruitful or be in danger of being laid aside.** Probably one of the reasons Jesus used this symbol is because the people of his day were familiar with crops and growing their own food.

The tie-in to the lesson is: if we are going to produce fruit in our lives, we need the help of the Holy Spirit.

1—Creative Writing

Materials: *Club 56 Activity Zone* page 24 and pens.

Note: This activity can be used to go along with the Outreach Project. However, if your class is not going to take part in the Outreach Project, the writing can be slightly modified and used on its own. The modifications are included in the lesson.

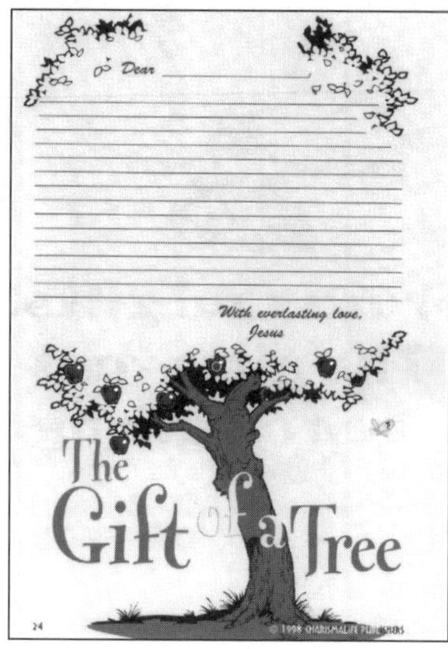

Activity Zone page 24

This week, we have talked about gifts to be used to serve God and the fruit that comes from walking with God. As part of our Outreach Project, we are going to serve others by giving them a gift of fruit trees to enjoy as they watch the trees grow, blossom and bear fruit. But we want to do more than just give them a nice tree to look at. We want to take this opportunity to tell them a little bit about the wonderful things that happen when you have a relationship with Christ. Just as the trees will bear apples, plums or cherries, so we will bear fruit in our lives when we know the Lord.

Ask the students to write a letter to the recipients of the trees as if the letter were written to them from God. If the students are participating in the Outreach Project, they can write the letter on the activity page. In the letters students should describe how their trees are examples of having a relationship with Christ. Also, they can describe the fruit that is produced in the lives of believers. Remind the students to convey the love that Jesus has for them.

These letters can be given to the people when the trees are planted. If the class will not be planting trees, a tree bearing fruit can be cut out of construction paper and taped on the classroom wall. Then the letters can be taped around the tree.

2—Cooking

Materials: *Club 56 Activity Zone* page 23, Bibles, pencils, kabob sticks (wooden), bowls (small), fruits (apples, peaches, grapes, blueberries, pineapple, pears, strawberries, watermelon, etc.), knife and napkins.

Before class: Cut the larger pieces of fruit into smaller chunks. Place the pieces in separate bowls.

Look at all these fruits I have brought to class. Are any of these your favorites?

Just as fruits are different, so are the fruits of the Spirit. The great news is the Holy Spirit makes all the fruits available to us.

Allow the students time to complete the questions.

Now we are going to assemble real fruit kabobs. You are free to choose whatever fruits you want to make up your kabob. Hopefully, though, you will want to sample all of the fruit that the Spirit offers us.

Activity Zone page 23

These cooking activities provide your class with some fun fellowship time. Fellowship is an important element in knitting your class together.

Fruits and gifts: The gifts that keep on giving.

Place the bowls on a table. Allow the students to assemble the fruit onto the wooden sticks. After they have put them together the way they want, allow them to eat and enjoy their creations.

3—Group Art

Materials: Construction paper (colored), scissors, markers, paper bag (small), tape (double-stick) and watch with second hand.

We have been learning about the fruit of the Spirit and the gifts that He gives. In our group project today we are going to concentrate on the fruit of the Spirit. Can you remember all nine of them?

Divide the class into small groups of five. Give each group the supplies listed above.

Your job is to come up with a real fruit that will represent each one of the fruits of the Spirit. For example, you might think a banana would best represent the quality of goodness. Once your group has decided on the fruits to represent each quality, each of you is to make a set of all nine fruits. On these fruits write the quality you have chosen it to represent.

When the students are done, regroup. **You have come up with some creative ideas to match the fruit of the Spirit with a real representation.**

Take all of the construction paper fruits that the students have created. Place them into the paper bag and mix them well. Have each student draw out nine pieces of fruit. (These will not be their own and there will also be repeats of qualities; that's OK.) Once the students each have nine fruits, have them tape the fruit to themselves.

We all want to have all of the fruit of the Spirit. As I look around, I see that right now not all of you have that. Some of you have several of the same qualities. Let's play a quick game to see if we can fix that situation.

Gather the students into a cleared area of the room. **You have one minute to try to collect all of the fruit that you need and get rid of any of the extra fruit that you have.**

Begin the game. The students are to remove from each other the fruit they need. They can also stick onto others any of their duplicate fruit. At the end of one minute see if any student was able to get all nine fruits of the Spirit.

4—Outreach Project

Materials: Fruit trees (several, small), potting soil, shovel (small), and watering can.

Note: If you are unable to obtain donations of fruit trees, check with members of your church to see if you can dig up some small shoots from fruit trees they may have in their yards.

In our exploration of the book of Galatians, we have been talking about the fruit of the Spirit that radiates from us as we become more like Christ. We have also talked about gifts that are given to us to be used to serve others. Club 56 is going to plan an activity that will incorporate both of these!

Our activity will include these three parts:

♦ We will choose a group of individuals to serve.

♦ We will go to their homes or businesses and plant fruit trees.

♦ We will give them letters explaining that the trees are symbols of the fruit of the Spirit (love, peace, joy, patience, kindness, goodness, faithfulness, gentleness and self-control) that are available to anyone who chooses to walk with Christ.

Listed below are several things to consider and plan for as you organize this outreach.

◊ Contact a nursery or garden store in your area. Ask if they would be willing to donate fruit trees and potting soil. Many stores would be happy to do this for a church group.

◊ Consider which trees would be most likely to grow in your climate. If you are located in an area with a cold climate and short growing season, you may be limited in your choices of trees that will bear fruit. Still, blossoming fruit trees will offer a good illustration for your students.

◊ Brainstorm with your students ideas of people for whom you could plant the trees. Suggestions include nursing homes, a Ronald McDonald house, Habitat for Humanity homes, inner-city neighborhoods or a new church being built in your area. Your students will be able to come up with other ideas.

◊ Decide as a class for whom you will plant the trees. Contact the people and plan a date and time.

◊ Gather adult volunteers to help drive and supervise the project. Check with your church to see if they have procedures you need to follow for outings (such as permission slips, insurance requirements for drivers, etc.)

◊ Complete the Creative Writing activity in Lesson 12 on *Club 56 Activity Zone* page 24. These letters will be given to the recipients of the trees.

Fruits and gifts: The gifts that keep on giving.

Materials: Copies of Living It Out story.

How could anyone ever call me selfish? Oh, I'm sorry, I should introduce myself. My name is Katie. I'm glad you're here. I need to tell someone what I'm going through with my mother.

I have this really great singing voice. Now before anyone gets heated, let me just tell you up front that I know it's a gift from God. But now I'm even writing some songs, and a lot of people at church and at school think they are really good. Just the other day one of my teachers said I remind her of Leann Rimes. Now what do you think of that? I could be incredibly famous.

I just wish my mom was as impressed as everyone else with all my talent. Do you know what she wants me to do? She wants me to go sing to a bunch of old people. Old people! Can you believe that? What would they know about the kind of music I sing?

When I told my mom that I wasn't going to waste my gift for singing on a bunch of fossils, she got so mad she left the room. When she started speaking to me again, she said she wasn't mad; she was disappointed! I think I like mad better because I really don't like to disappoint my folks. But my mom needs to see that I am a "bright new vocal talent." That's the way the guy introduced me at the Talent Search when I sang for them.

I told Mom that I needed to use all my free time writing songs and performing for people who can help advance my career. No matter what, I'll still always sing for the Lord in my spare time. Of course I don't have a lot of spare time.

Now how can my mom think I'm selfish? Can you see anything in what I've said that seems at all selfish? I'm just being realistic. Mom says that the fruit of the Spirit needs to be evident in my life. Well, I think all of my talents are evidence that the fruit of the Spirit is active in my life, don't you?

Why don't you look over what I've told you and get back to me? Just a note will do because I'm going to be pretty busy writing new songs. Thanks.

What should Katie do?

Divide the class into small discussion groups. Give each group a copy of the story. Ask them to consider what Katie has said and answer her questions. When they have finished, have them share their responses with the class.

Materials: Copies of Lesson 12 Secret Orders.

In the God game, the Holy Spirit gives you all of these gifts and fruit that help you live your life in the right way. In the spy game, we have to rely on the scientists in our secret labs to come up with tricky devices that help us through our mission.

Your secret orders for this week are to design some kind of device that a secret agent can use but also one that would employ one of the fruits of the Spirit. For example, maybe you would come up with a fountain pen that would squirt a dose of goodness into the face of an evil enemy, thus converting him into a good guy. See what I mean?

Go to work. You have one week to come up with your device.

Remember to bring your completed Secret Orders to class next week.

SECRET ORDERS

Design some kind of device that a secret agent can use that would employ one of the fruit of the Spirit.

Introducing the latest New Kids' tracts ———————

New Kids' Guide to
Supernatural Encounters

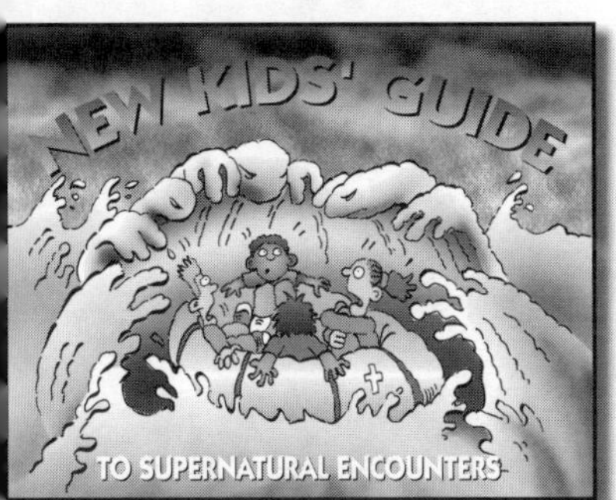

Are Ouija Boards OK? What's wrong with reading horoscopes...after all, everyone's doing it. Today more than ever, your kids are bombarded with New Age and demonic practices. This full-color guide will give kids a clear foundation and understanding of some of the most common New Age and demonic practices they may encounter in their schools and with friends. For grades 3–6.

New Kids' Guide to
Sharing Jesus

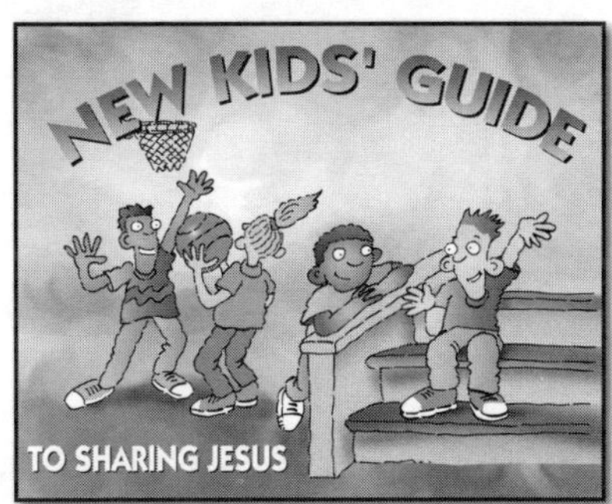

How do you teach children to witness? Now, with this colorful booklet, you can present kids with an easy-to-follow plan for understanding the importance of sharing their faith with others and simple ways to get started.

Our original best-selling New Kids' tracts ———————

New Kid in the Kingdom

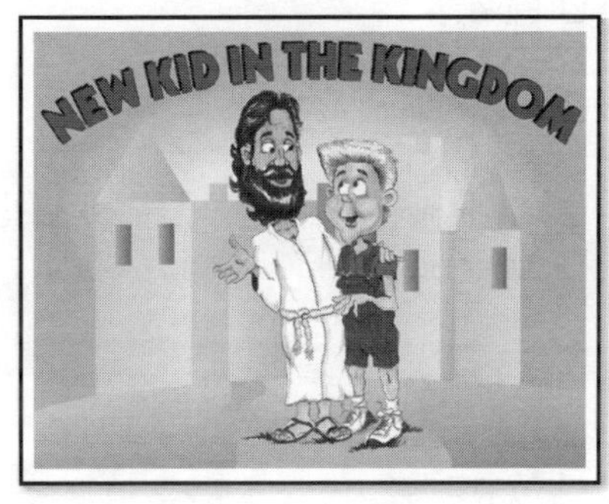

Bright, colorful, easy-to-understand booklet that tells how to be Jesus' friend, how sin separates us from Him and how to receive eternal life. Order in quantities to hand out during your Sunday School, Children's Church or Vacation Bible School.

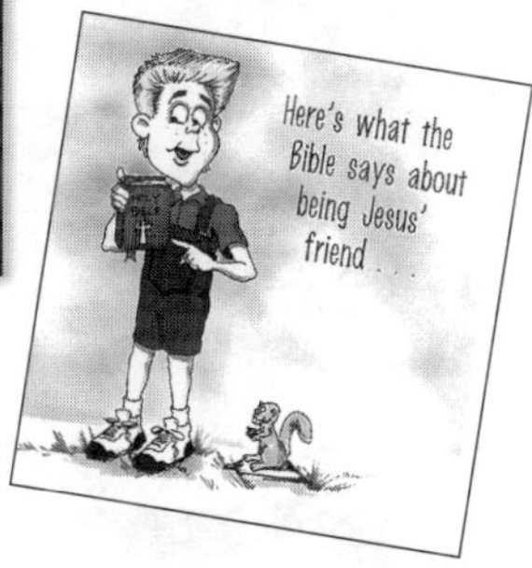

New Kid in the Spirit

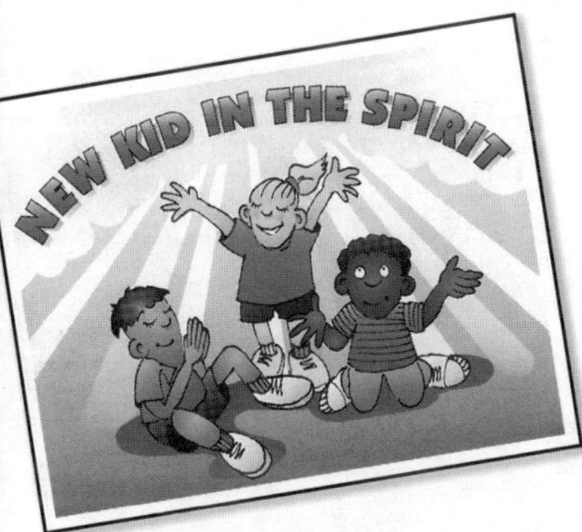

You'll appreciate this step-by-step guide with full-color illustrations on how to lead a child into the baptism in the Holy Spirit and into a daily walk in the fullness of His power.

To order, call

1-800-451-4598

Tract prices:

10-packs	$ 7.95	(80¢ each)
25-packs	$17.95	(72¢ each)
100-packs	$54.95	(55¢ each)

ITEMS NEEDED FOR LESSON

challenge review

- ❏ Challenge notebooks
- ❏ Lesson 12 Secret Orders

opening activity

- ❏ Index cards
- ❏ Pencils
- ❏ Seeds (apple, pumpkin, sunflower, lemon [or orange], watermelon and popcorn)
- ❏ Products of seeds (apple, pumpkin, sunflower, lemon [or orange], watermelon and popcorn)

bible lesson

- ❏ Bibles
- ❏ Root beer (2-liter bottles)
- ❏ Cups (plastic)
- ❏ Spoons
- ❏ Ice cream (vanilla)
- ❏ Ice cream scoop

memory verse activity

- ❏ Scissors
- ❏ Posterboard
- ❏ Magazines
- ❏ Glue

living it out

- ❏ None

more activities

1—Music

- ❏ *Club 56 Activity Zone* page 25
- ❏ Pencils

2—Group Art

- ❏ *Club 56 Activity Zone* page 26
- ❏ Markers (colored)
- ❏ Scissors
- ❏ Tape

3—Bible Study

- ❏ Popcorn (unpopped, one bag)
- ❏ Permanent markers (red, blue, green, orange and purple)
- ❏ Bowl (small)
- ❏ Tweezers
- ❏ Construction paper (red, orange, blue, green and purple)
- ❏ Tape
- ❏ Bibles

4—Problem Solving

- ❏ Index cards (32)
- ❏ Bibles
- ❏ Pen
- ❏ Tape

challenge for the week

- ❏ Copies of Lesson 13 Secret Orders

SPECIAL NOTE

As you complete this quarter take time to go over the evaluation on the inside cover of the *Club 56 Activity Zone* with your students. When you complete it, send it to: CharismaLife Publishers, Attn: Product Development, 600 Rinehart Road, Lake Mary, Florida 32746.

Likewise, review the Power Points and Memory Verses by using the activities on pages 27 and 28 of the *Club 56 Activity Zone* books.

Forever freedom comes from following the Father.

We must not become tired of doing good. We will receive our harvest of eternal life at the right time. We must not give up!

Galatians 6:9

See Bible Lesson for Scripture References

A. Mission Impossible

B. Back to the Future

C. Be Prepared . . . I'll Be Back

LIFE WITH CHRIST: FROM HERE TO ETERNITY

It was a glorious fall day. The air was crisp but still warm enough to coax me into the great outdoors. Everywhere up and down 6th Street, which at that time was almost my entire world, the leaves had fallen from the trees. Great piles of them were mounded on the lawn and proved too tempting for my 8-year-old sensibilities. Jumping into the nearest pile and throwing leaves into the air, I thoroughly enjoyed myself. Finally exhausted, I crashed into another large pile. As I lay there breathing in the scents of fall, I felt utterly content. All was right in my small world.

My gaze turned up to the beautiful blue sky. Passing across in a slow motion march was a group of puffy white clouds. Quite suddenly a thought popped into my head: *Maybe today is the day Jesus will come back. Maybe He will come right now, at this very moment. He might be waiting up there on one of those clouds, unseen until His grand entrance.* Hope swelled in my heart and I found myself praying, "Please come, Jesus."

Since the time of the early church, that is the same collective prayer that all believers have been praying. Jesus who came once to save the world, has promised to come again to collect all of His followers. Though it is yet to happen, we have much to anticipate.

As you finish up the book of Galatians, remind your class of this hope. It is because Jesus is alive and coming again that we live as we do. It is the event that all of the church anticipates.

Materials: Challenge notebooks and Lesson 12 Secret Orders.

Have students share their inventions for getting the fruit of the Spirit to others. Have them place their completed Secret Orders in their Challenge notebooks.

Materials: Index cards, pencils and seeds (apple, pumpkin, sunflower, lemon [or orange], watermelon and popcorn) and products of seeds (apple, pumpkin, sunflower, lemon [or orange], watermelon and popcorn).

Before class: Place the different types of seeds on the index cards. Label each index card with a number. Place the fruits and vegetables out of sight of the children.

Are you good at recognizing objects? I hope so because I am going to ask you to identify some seeds for me. Some of them may be familiar to you, others might not. Let's see how many you can get right. Hand out the index cards and pencils. Lay out the seed examples. Ask the students to write numbers on their index cards and then to write the correct answer by their guesses. When they are finished, reveal what the correct answers are for each seed card.

That was pretty easy, wasn't it? Most of the seeds we looked at were ones that we are familiar with. Now I want you to think about what these seeds become or grow in to. Bring out the grown examples that you have brought. These certainly don't resemble the seeds they grew from, do they? The seeds were put into the ground, we didn't see them for a while and then—surprise—they reappeared in a new form. Our lesson today is about a promise that Jesus gave us. He told us (Matt. 26:64) that He would come again in a way different from His first coming. Read the verse to the class.

♦ What are some of the differences the verse tells us about?

The second coming of Jesus is mentioned over 300 times in the New Testament. Paul talks about it around 50 times in his different letters. Obviously, it was an important theme and hope of the early Church. Well, all of this sounds great, you may be saying to yourself, but what does it have to do with me and what in the world does it have to do with our activity about seeds?

♦ How do the seeds remind us about Jesus' second coming?

Just as the seeds had to be planted into the ground to change and bear fruit, so Jesus died, rose and will return. Only this time His return is going to be really something to witness, not like His quiet birth in a small stable.

Get involved

The opening activity is an important part of the lesson. Be sure to include it. It will set the focus for the rest of the lesson.

Forever freedom comes from following the Father.

Materials: Bibles, root beer (2-liter bottles), cups (plastic), spoons, ice cream (vanilla) and ice cream scoop.

Mission Impossible

♦ Are you wondering why Jesus had to come two different times? I mean why didn't He just do everything the first time He came? *(Allow for some discussion time.)*

Let's take a look at some of the reasons for Jesus' first coming. *(Have the students look up the following verses. Ask for volunteers to read the verses out loud.)*

◊ Matthew 1:21   ◊ Luke 19:10   ◊ John 3:17

◊ John 10:9-11   ◊ John 12:47

These verses reveal to us that Jesus had a specific mission the first time He came to earth.

♦ What was Jesus' mission?

♦ How did He accomplish His mission?

♦ Do you consider Jesus' mission a success?

Jesus was sent to earth to bring the gift of salvation to us all. He offered Himself as the sacrifice and atonement for our sins. He made a way for us to be made right once again with our Father. That was Jesus' first mission.

However, that was not to be Jesus' only mission. While He was here the first time, He even spoke about His return mission. He told us that the next time He comes, it will be for a different purpose. Let's see if we can find out what Jesus' next mission is to be.

◊ Matthew 16:27   ◊ Matthew 25:31-32   ◊ 1 Corinthians. 4:5

◊ 2 Timothy 4:1   ◊ Jude 1:14-15

♦ How does Jesus' second coming different in purpose from His first?

♦ What will Jesus' second coming accomplish?

Jesus came the first time to give us the gift of salvation. His return will be to gather those who have accepted His gift and believe in Him. I think Hebrews 9:28 says it best. *(Read this verse to the class out loud.)*

Back to the Future

We know that Jesus has promised to return. We have also learned that His return will be different from His first. We know He is going to gather His followers, but when will this be? What else do we know about Jesus' second coming? *(Ask the students to contribute any information they know about Jesus' return.)*

Let's find out what the Bible has to tell us about Jesus' second coming. *(Have the students look up the following verses. Ask for volunteers to read the verses out loud.)*

◊ Matthew 24:27
◊ Luke 12:40
◊ Hebrews 10:37
◊ Revelation 3:11
◊ 1 Peter 5:4

◊ Matthew 24:36
◊ 1 Thessalonians 5:2
◊ James 5:8
◊ John 14:31
◊ 1 John 3:2

♦ **What are some of the things the Bible tells us about Jesus' return?** *That the time of His return is unknown. We should be prepared. His coming is near.*

♦ **Do you believe that Jesus' coming is at hand?**

♦ **Would you be prepared for Jesus to come tomorrow?**

♦ **How does knowing that Jesus will return affect you?**

We don't know when Jesus is going to return, but we do know that He promised us He would. Until that happens, we should live our lives in such a way as to be prepared for when He comes again.

Be Prepared...I'll Be Back

So, what are we to do in the meantime? Does Jesus mean for us to just sit around and try our best to stay out of trouble?

Here is where we can take a lesson from the Boy Scouts and their motto, "Be prepared."

♦ **If you knew you were going to spend an entire day at the beach, what would you take to go prepared? How about a day of skiing in the mountains?**

Just as we would get ready for any activity that we were going to do, we should also be ready for the Lord's return. The question is, how do we do that?

♦ **What are some of things we can do to be ready?**

(Have a discussion with the students. Allow them to come up with the practical things that they, as 5th and 6th graders, can do. Try to encourage them to go beyond the simple basics such as reading the Bible and praying. Encourage them to think of everyday things that will keep their relationship with God growing.)

Our study in Galatians has offered us many ways to grow in our relationship with God. Now you have come up with some that are personal to you. We want to continue adding these kinds of applications to our faith to ensure that our relationship with God keeps on growing.

Let me demonstrate to you just what I mean. *(Scoop some ice cream into a cup. Pour root beer on top of it. Encourage the students to watch it foam.)* This ice cream changed when we added the root beer to it. As you continue in your faith, you, too, will be changed. You will grow to be more like Jesus. Then someday He will return to take us all home. *(Make a root beer float for each of the students. Enjoy a time of fun and fellowship as you end your study of Galatians.)*

Many of the students' answers to the questions may be more their opinion than fact. It is good to allow for freedom in your classroom, but make sure you are always standing firm in the standards of the Bible. Gently point students to the sure Word of God.

Forever freedom comes from following the Father.

Galatians 6:9

We must not become tired of doing good. We will receive our harvest of eternal life at the right time. We must not give up!

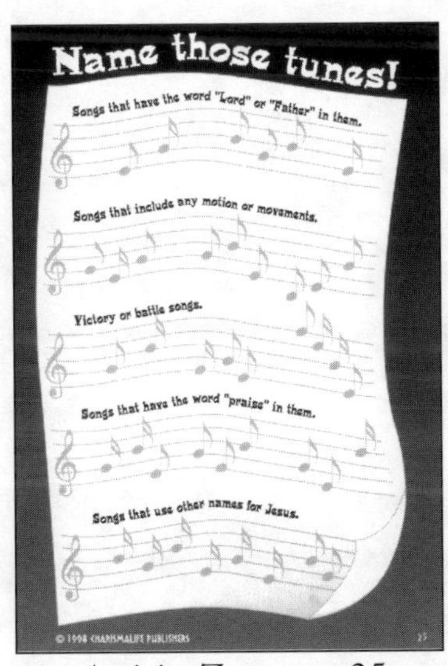

Activity Zone page 25

Conclusion

In our study of Galatians, we have learned about many of the freedoms that God gives us. Ultimately, we know that true freedom comes from following our Father—and that means someday we will even follow Him into heaven.

Materials: Scissors, posterboard, magazines and glue.

Have any of you ever been on a scavenger hunt? Do you know what one is? Allow for some discussion. If the students don't know what one is, explain that it is a hunt for different items that are on a list.

We are going to go on a scavenger hunt today, but we aren't going to leave the classroom. In this hunt, we are going to try to locate items (pictures) that will remind us about our Memory Verse.

Divide the class into small groups. Give each group the supply materials.

You will need to work as a group to come up with the actual words that are in the Memory Verse or picture representations. For example, the word *time* might be represented with a picture of a clock or a watch. For the word *harvest*, you might find a picture of a field of grain or a garden. Remember, you can always look for the actual printed word. When you have completed the entire verse, glue it to the posterboard in the correct order. Be ready to share your finished product with the class when you are done.

After the groups have finished, regroup and have them display their picture verse. Then have each group recite the verse together.

1—Music

Materials: *Club 56 Activity Zone* page 25 and pencils.

Did you know that when you put anything to music, it is easier to remember? Think of all the silly jingles and commercials that are floating around in your head. Hopefully, along with all of those songs, there are also some Christian worship songs. You are going to need to remember as many of those songs as you can to help your team win in our game today.

Hand out the activity pages. Allow the students five minutes to work and to come up with as many song titles as they can. At the end of the time, bring the class back together and divide them into equal teams. (If your class is large, you may want to have more than two teams.)

Each song group on the sheet counts as one round. Begin with one team naming a song that fits the first category. Allow each team to continue naming other songs, receiving a point for each song the team members come up with, until one of the teams is stumped. The team that was last able to come up with a song title wins five points for that round. Continue on with the other categories on the worksheet. When all the rounds have been played, tally up the scores and declare the winning team.

2—Group Art

Materials: *Club 56 Activity Zone* page 26, markers (colored), scissors and tape.

Note: Bring in actual quilts if possible.

Long ago women gathered to make quilts. Many times the patterns or fabrics that were used would tell a story or help commemorate a special event.

For the last several months we have been studying the book of Galatians. In it we have discovered many of the wonderful gifts and freedoms that God offers to us. As you think back over the last several weeks, what lesson or event spoke the loudest to you? Take some time to review many of the concepts in the past 13 lessons.

Just as the quilters would gather to work together, I am going to ask each one of you to design and color a square that tells about something you have learned about during our study of Galatians. When you are done with your square, we will cut it out and tape it with all the others to form a Galatians' quilt. We can then hang it in our room to help us remember the lessons we have learned.

When the students are done, cut out the squares and tape them together. Hang the finished Galatians' quilt on the wall in your Club 56 room.

3—Bible Study

Materials: Popcorn (unpopped, one bag), permanent markers (red, blue, green, orange and purple), bowl (small), tweezers, construction paper (red, orange, blue, green and purple), tape and Bibles.

Before class: Take five popcorn seeds. With permanent markers, color one red, one blue, one green, one orange and one purple. Then write one of the following verses on each sheet of construction paper: Job 17:9, John 15:7, Hebrews 12:1, 1 Peter 1:13 and Revelation 3:11. Pour all of the popcorn seeds into a bowl, including the colored ones.

You finish a huge lunch that your mom packed for you and then head off for PE class. When you get into the gym, your teacher announces that everyone will have to run a mile. You will be timed to see how fast you can do it. ▼

Activity Zone page 26

Forever freedom comes from following the Father.

You feel good in the beginning, but as the race continues, you start to struggle. You have a terrible side ache from eating before you ran. Also, your legs are starting to hurt. After running for what seems like hours, you hear your teacher yell, "Keep going. You're halfway there!" Halfway! You don't think you can make it. You are ready to quit.

♦ Have you ever felt like quitting? What did you want to quit?

Our Memory Verse encourages us to not become tired of doing good or give up. We are encouraged to persevere. Even when it gets hard and seems hopeless, we are to keep trying! We are going to find some other places in the Bible that encourage us to persevere. To find the verses that you will read, you are going to have to persevere a little bit, too!

Have the students sit in a circle. Give the bowl of popcorn seeds and tweezers to one student. He will have five seconds to use the tweezers to pick up one colored seed. If he misses, he will pass the bowl to the next person. If he is successful, he will be given the paper that is the same color as the popcorn seed. He will then tape the paper to the wall and the class will look up the verse written on the paper. The bowl will continue to be passed around the circle until all five colored seeds have been found and the five verses have been read. After all the verses have been read, discuss the following questions:

♦ What do all of the verses have in common?

♦ What can we do if we feel like giving up?

4—Problem Solving

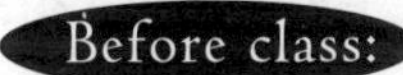

Materials: Index cards (32), Bibles, pens and tape.

Before class: On index cards, write each of the situations and verses below (eight total). Then, make three more sets of the same eight cards:

◊ Your friend is a Christian, but he is getting into all kinds of trouble at school. He has started stealing and cheating. He says it doesn't matter because God forgives him.

◊ Galatians 5:13

◊ A girl in your church says she is confused. She is not sure what she believes anymore. She used to believe that she was saved because she had a personal relationship with Jesus. Then some people came to her door and told her that she'd better make sure she doesn't sin or she won't go to heaven.

◊ Galatians 1:9

◊ You are trying to walk with the Lord, but sometimes it gets hard. You feel like giving up.

◊ Galatians 6:9

◊ A friend asks you how you could tell if someone was a Christian just by looking at his life.

◊ Galatians 5:22–23

As we wrap up our study of the book of Galatians, we can look back over many great verses we memorized. Now, when we face some difficult situations we have words from God to guide us.

Divide the class into four groups. Give each group a package of index cards prepared before class. **Your group has been given four cards with short situations written on them. You also have been given four cards with some of this quarter's Memory Verses written on them. It is your group's task to match one situation with the verse that would help solve the problem. When you think you have them all matched, tape them on the wall so the verse is directly across from the situation.**

After all the groups have discussed the problems and matched them with the verses that offer solutions, discuss the following questions:

♦ Did all four groups match the verses in the same way? If not, which were different?

♦ If you were faced with these problems, would the verses help you solve them? How?

Discuss each situation again, asking for volunteers to say how they would respond.

Jake sat down in frustration as he watched his mom talk to his teacher. Naturally, he would be blamed for the whole thing. His mother came over to his desk. "Get your things, Jake, we need to catch the bus." Her voice was almost emotionless as she helped him slide his books into the backpack. "Jake, you have to learn to control your temper. Mr. Brink said that he understands you were provoked into this fight, but he also said that you totally lost control and hurt Mannie." Jake couldn't think of anything to say. He shuffled along beside his mom wishing that he had just walked away from Mannie's taunts. *Why did he always get so angry?*

At home that afternoon he watched his mother fold laundry. Neither of them spoke for a long time. At last his mother looked up from her work. "Jake, I love you, and I'm sad that you're having a difficult time. But I want you to know that Jesus loves you and He wants you to bring your problems to Him. He will help you."

Jake looked down. "You know what, Mom?" he asked softly. "I don't know if it's even worth it to be a Christian. I've asked over and over for Jesus to help me, and I just keep messing up. Maybe he just doesn't want to help me." Jake's mom put the sheet she was folding on the table and went to sit by him.

"Oh, honey, He does want to help you and He will. Jesus has promised to give you the strength and courage you need to help you through difficult times. Let's just talk to Him right now, OK?" Jake wasn't sure he wanted to pray. Sensing his hesitation, his mom spoke. "You know, Jake, when Jesus sets us free, He does it completely. Sometimes He helps us see why we do the things we do. It helps us appreciate the work He does in our hearts. Why don't you think about that a little while I put the laundry away? When I come back we can talk a little more."

Alone, Jake put his head down on the table. More than anything he wanted to be in control of his temper. He really did want to be free. But was it just too hard?

Forever freedom comes from following the Father.

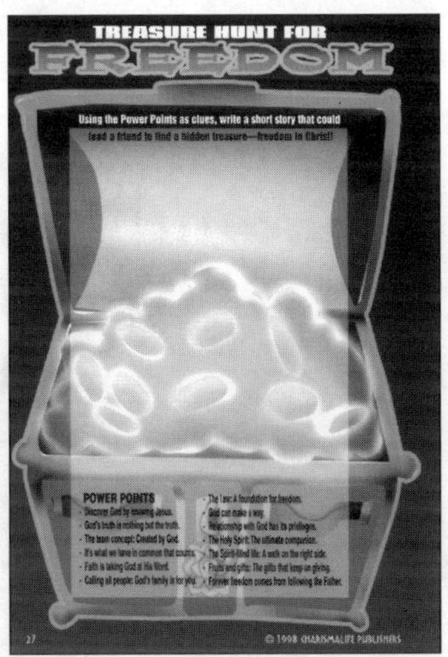

Activity Zone page 27

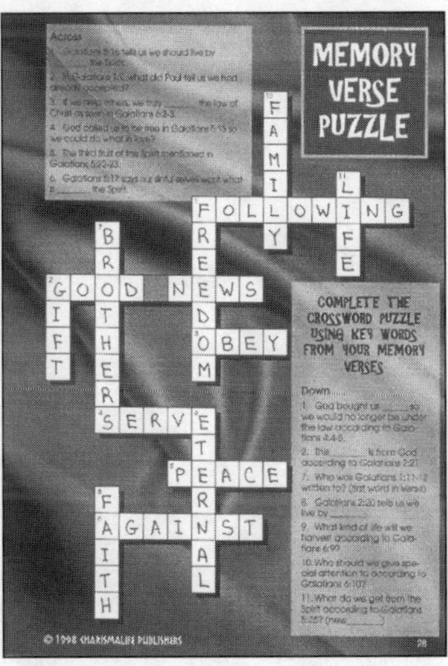

Activity Zone page 28

What can Jake do?

Divide the class into small discussion groups. Read the Memory Verse for today to the class and them have them discuss the following questions:

- ◆ Why did Jake get into a scuffle with Mannie?
- ◆ Why was Jake discouraged about his anger?
- ◆ What did Jake's mother say that Jesus has promised His people?
- ◆ If Jake came to you for advice, what would you tell him?

Materials: Copies of Lesson 13 Secret Orders.

All of our missions have a beginning and an end. We are given the assignment, we go out into the field to do the work and hopefully we are able to stop the bad guys. Sometimes it works and sometimes we have to mark the mission a failure.

This week your challenge is to think of your life as a mission. Make a time line. Mark the beginning with your birth. Then mark some points along the way—things that have been a success in your life. Some of the things that you might want to include would be the day you came to know Jesus or the day you got baptized. Another day may be a success you experienced in school or at a sporting event. Other important things might be memorizing Scripture or the time you shared the Good News with a friend. Try to come up with as many "success" points as you can. Then at the end of the your lifeline, you can mark a spot for joining God in heaven. Even though we may not know exactly where our lives are going, if we walk with Jesus, we do know how they are going to end.

Good luck! Think hard! You have done great work as a secret agent. Your talents and gifts will serve you well as you work to complete the missions ahead of you.

Give each student their Challenge notebook to take home. Encourage them to complete this week's assignment and share it with a friend or family member.

Quarter Review

Materials: *Club 56 Activity Zone* pages 27 and 28 and pencils.

How many of you remember our Power Points and Memory Verses from this quarter? Have the students divide into pairs to complete pages 27 and 28. Read the directions as a group and then allow them to complete the activities in class.

SECRET ORDERS
Your final secret order is to think of your life as a mission. Make a time line beginning with your birth and continuing to your final destination—heaven—if you have received Christ. Fill it in with important dates and events that have already happened in your life. Even though you don't know what is to come, if you are walking with Jesus, you do know how it is going to end.